ECCLESIOGENESIS

ECCLESIOGENESIS

The Base Communities Reinvent the Church

LEONARDO BOFF

Translated from the Portuguese by
Robert R. Barr

ORBIS BOOKS
Maryknoll, New York 10545

Fifth Printing, September 1997

Originally published as *Eclesiogênese: As comunidades eclesiais de base reinventam a Igreja*, by Editora Vozes Ltda., Rua Frei Luís, 100, 25.600, Petrópolis, RJ, Brazil. Copyright © 1977 Instituto Nacional de Pastoral (da CNBB). Chapter 4 was originally published as "Comunidades Eclesiais de Base: povo oprimido que se organiza para a libertaçao," *Revista Eclesiástica Brasileira* 41, June 1981, pp. 312–320. Chapter 6 was originally published as a pamphlet (Vozes imprint) entitled *O coordenador leigo e a Celebração da ceia do Senhor*

English translation © 1986 by Orbis Books, Maryknoll, NY 10545

Manuscript editor: Lisa McGaw

Library of Congress Cataloging in Publication Data

Boff, Leonardo.
   Ecclesiogenesis: the base communities reinvent the church.

   Bibliography: p.
   Includes index.
   1. Christian communities—Catholic Church.
2. Church renewal—Catholic Church. 3. Church.
4. Lord's Supper—Lay celebration. 5. Women clergy.
6. Catholic Church—Doctrines. 7. Catholic Church—
Government. 8. Catholic Church—Clergy. 9. Lord's
Supper—Catholic Church. 10. Liberation theology.
I. Title.
BX2347.5.B63 1986   262'.02   85-15600
ISBN 0–88344–214–0 (pbk.)

To Bishop Luís Fernandes
of Vitória, Espírito Santo,
for his talent for hearing what the Spirit has to say
to the churches through God's People

Contents

ECCLESIOGENESIS

A New Experience of Church

Modern society has produced a wild atomization of existence and a general anonymity of persons lost in the cogs of the mechanisms of the macro-organizations and bureaucracies. These massive structures produce uniformity—uniformity of behavior, of societal framework, of schedules and timetables, and so on. But there has been a reaction. Slowly, but with ever-increasing intensity, we have witnessed the creation of communities in which persons actually know and recognize one another, where they can be themselves in their individuality, where they can "have their say," where they can be welcomed by name. And so, we see, groups and little communities have sprung up everywhere. This phenomenon exists in the church, as well: grassroots Christian communities, as they are known, or basic church communities.

The Basic Church Community

Through the latter centuries, the church has acquired an organizational form with a heavily hierarchical framework and a juridical understanding of relationships among Christians, thus producing mechanical, reified inequalities and inequities. As Yves Congar has written: "Think of the church as a huge organization, controlled by a hierarchy, with subordinates whose only task it is to keep the rules and follow the practices. Would this be a caricature? Scarcely!"[1]

In reaction, the basic church communities have sprung up. They represent a new experience of church, of community, of communion of persons within the more legitimate (in the strict sense of the word) ancient tradition. It would be simplistic and would betray the lack of a sense of history to conceive of the basic church communities as a purely contingent, transitory phenomenon. They represent "a specific response to a prevailing historical conjuncture."[2] Theologically they signify a new ecclesiological experience, a renaissance of very church, and hence an action of the Spirit on the horizon of the matters urgent for our time.[3] Seen in this way, the basic church communities deserve to be contemplated, welcomed, and respected as salvific events. Not that we are

1

thereby dispensed from a diligent quest for lucidity and for better ways. Our every effort at comprehension is called for, as we undertake a theological contemplation of the eminent ecclesial value of these communities.

Within this more general frame of reference, however, we are also moved by more specific considerations of the actual situation of the church and its new awareness. The rise of the basic communities is also due to the crisis in the church institution. The scarcity of ordained ministers to attend to the needs of these communities has aroused the creative imagination of the pastors themselves, and they have come to entrust the laity with more and more responsibility. Although the great majority of basic church communities owe their origin to a priest or a member of a religious order, they nevertheless basically constitute a lay movement. The laity carry forward the cause of the gospel here, and are the vessels, the vehicles of ecclesial reality even on the level of direction and decision-making. This shift of the ecclesial axis contains, in seed, a new principle for "birthing the church," for "starting the church again."[4] It is a transposition that bids fair to form the principle of a genuine "ecclesiogenesis"—to use a word that was employed on several occasions in the Vitória dialogue of January 1975. We are not dealing with the expansion of an existing ecclesiastical system, rotating on a sacramental, clerical axis, but with the emergence of another form of being church, rotating on the axis of the word and the laity. We may well anticipate that, from this movement, of which the universal church is becoming aware, a new type of institutional presence of Christianity in the world may now come into being.

A new phenomenon creates its own language and establishes its own categories for coming to self-expression. The phenomenon of the basic communities constitutes no exception to this rule. The basic communities are generating a new ecclesiology, formulating new concepts in theology. This is still just beginning, still in process. It is not accomplished reality. Pastors and theologians, take warning! Respect the new way that is appearing on the horizon. Do not seek at once to box this phenomenon within theological-pastoral categories distilled from other contexts and other ecclesial experiences. Instead, assume the attitude of those who would see, understand, and learn. Maintain a critical watchfulness, and help us to discern true paths from false. The history of the church is not merely the history of the actualization of ancient forms or of a return to the pristine experiences of the historical past. The history of the church is genuine history: the creation of never-before-experienced novelty. Even the New Testament, like the history of the church, presents a pluriform institutional incarnation of the faith. The church's path from Christ's first coming to the Parousia is not rectilinear. It moves through historical variations, carrying the world through different ages, and offers it to God. Perhaps we are now in a phase of the emergence of a new institutional type of church. Our situation will have to be understood in the light of the Holy Spirit. We must conquer our mental resistance, modify our church habits, and stay open. Otherwise we may smother the Spirit.

A vast spectrum of questions is tied up with the subject of the basic communities. We can hope to list only the most pressing ones, and so we shall select those that seem to be the most significant: the ecclesiality of these communities, their contribution to a transcendence of the church's current structure and, as *quaestiones disputatae*, the historical Jesus and the institutional forms of the church, the possibility of a lay person celebrating the Lord's Supper, and women's priesthood and its possibilities. Before moving on to these questions, however, let us briefly survey the emergence and inherent possibilities of basic church communities.

"Building a Living Church"

The emergence of the basic church communities in Brazil began with a community evangelization movement in Barra do Pirai, R.J. (Rio de Janeiro district) and the efforts of lay catechists there.[5] Specific concerns were with a movement for grassroots community catechetics and general education via radio, from Natal, R.J., and various lay apostolate experiments and parish renewal within the framework of a renewal movement projected in the national pastoral plans (1962–65). One of the plans recounts these beginnings:

In 1956 Dom Agnelo Rossi initiated an evangelization movement, using lay catechists, for regions of Brazil not being reached by pastors. It all began with the lament of one humble old woman: "Christmas Eve, all three Protestant churches were lit up and full of people. We could hear them singing. . . . And the Catholic church, closed and dark! . . . Because we can't get a priest." A question hung in the air. If there are no priests, must everything grind to a halt? At this juncture, Dom Agnelo, in Barra do Pirai, decided to train community coordinators "to do everything a lay person can do in God's church in current ecclesiastical discipline. At the least, these catechists will gather the people once a week for religious instruction. Normally they will also celebrate daily prayer with the people. On Sundays and Holy Days they will gather the people from all over the district for a 'Massless Sunday,' or 'priestless Mass,' or 'Catholic worship,' and lead them spiritually and collectively in the same Mass as is being celebrated by the pastor in the distant mother church. They will recite morning and evening prayers with the people, as well as novenas, litanies, May and June celebrations, and so on" (*Revista Eclesiástica Brasileira* 17 [1957]:731–37). Thus catechesis became the center of a community, and someone was responsible for religious life. Instead of chapels, meeting halls were built and then used for school, religious instruction, sewing lessons, and meetings for solving community problems, even economic ones.
    To deal with grave human problems of illiteracy, epidemic, and so on, "radio schools" were created, along with the MEB (Movement for Basic Education), in Natal, for the archdiocese. Reading and writing, along with other school subjects and, of course, religion, were taught by radio. On Sundays, communities without a priest would gather around the radio and

pray aloud the people's parts of the Mass being celebrated by the bishop, and hear his homily. By 1963 there were 1,410 radio schools in the country *REB* 23 [1963]:781). By then the movement had spread all over the north-east and centerwest.

The Better World Movement created an atmosphere of renewal through-out the country. A team of fifteen persons traveled about the country for five years, giving 1,800 courses and stimulating all areas of church life. Priests, bishops, religious, laity, and movements all experienced this re-newal. This program resulted in the Brazilian Bishops' Conference's Emer-gency Plan, and the First Nationwide Pastoral Plan (1965-70), which said, in part: "Our present parishes are or ought to be composed of various local communities and 'basic communities,' in view of their great extent, popula-tion density, and percentage of persons baptized and hence juridically belonging to them. It will be of great importance, then, to launch a parish renewal in each place, for the creation and ongoing dynamics of these 'basic communities.' The mother church will itself gradually become one of these communities, and the pastor will preside in all of them, because all are to be found in the portion of the Lord's flock with which he has been entrusted."[6]

Ever since the Medellín conference (1968) this new ecclesial reality has been winning its citizenship, and today it constitutes, without a doubt, one of the great principles of church renewal worldwide.[7] The basic communities mean "building a living church rather than multiplying material structures."[8] The communities are built on a more vital, lively, intimate participation in a more or less homogeneous entity, as their members seek to live the essence of the Christian message: the universal parenthood of God, communion with all human beings, the following of Jesus Christ who died and rose again, the celebration of the resurrection and the Eucharist, and the upbuilding of the kingdom of God, already under way in history as the liberation of the whole human being and all human beings.

Christian life in the basic communities is characterized by the absence of alienating structures, by direct relationships, by reciprocity, by a deep commu-nion, by mutual assistance, by communality of gospel ideals, by equality among members. The specific characteristics of society are absent here: rigid rules; hierarchies; prescribed relationships in a framework of a distinction of functions, qualities, and titles. The enthusiasm generated by a community life of interpersonal ties, and the experience of breathing the fulfilling atmosphere of the gospel frequently lead to a problem that is not without its gravity. Pastors should be attentive here, and not succumb to illusions. The question is: May the basic church communities be seen as an alternative to the church as such? Or less audaciously: May one arouse and nourish the expectation that the whole church may one day be transformed into a community? What degree of probability may we ascribe to this expectation? Can the entire church in its globalism be transformed into authentic community?

In order to develop a response to this question, theology must listen to what the "social sciences"—or better, the sciences of the social—have to say from their meditation on the relation between communitarian and societal aspects of human life. Here we have help in sociologist Pedro Demo's most competent study on the "sociological problems of community."[9] Sociology today has gone beyond F. Tönnies's classic contrast between society and community. For Tönnies, *a community is a social formation in which human beings are oriented by a sense of reciprocity and "belonging"; a society, by contrast, is a social formation in which anonymity and indirect relationships prevail.* This is not to deny that there are social formations whose relationships are based on a communitarian spirit—on intimate, direct, trusting, informal, reciprocal, egalitarian contact, with a maximum of exchange, interchange, and equivalency. Still, in concrete history, no social formation, not even in the presence of these values, has ever succeeded in extinguishing all traces of conflict, selfishness, individualism, individual and group interest, the pressure to have order and rules, and the establishment of goals with a rigid process for their attainment.

Community does not constitute a typical phase of human-group formation. Nor is it possible for community to exist in a pure state. Concretely, there is always a power structure, in either the dominative or the solidarity version. There are always inequalities and stratified roles, in function of some particular scale of values. There are conflicts and particular interests. Historically, social formations are mixed: they have some societal and some communitarian characteristics. Thus in a certain sense, it is unrealistic to struggle for a "classless society"—a society that would be simply and totally a community of brothers and sisters, without any conflict at all. Realistically, one can only struggle for a type of sociability in which love will be less difficult, and where power and participation will have better distribution. Community must be understood as a spirit to be created, as an inspiration to bend one's constant efforts to overcome barriers between persons and to generate a relationship of solidarity and reciprocity.

As Demo well says: "In terms of the relationship of community to society, community can be said to be society's utopia."[10] Human togetherness will always be charged with tensions between the "organizational impersonal" and the "intimate personal." A struggle for the supremacy of the communitarian dimension implies a struggle to prevent structures and grades from becoming substantive, a struggle to see that they assist the humanization of the human being, and thus bring human beings ever nearer to one another and to the values of the gospel. The supremacy of the communitarian over the societal comes more easily in small groups. Hence the importance of the basic church communities. They are communities within church society.

In order to maintain its vitality as a force for renewal, the communitarian spirit stands in constant need of nourishment and stimulation. Simply for the faithful to be together in the execution of certain tasks is not enough. Clubs and other associations do this, but are not considered communities for it. What constitutes a human group as a community is the effort to create and maintain community involvement as an ideal, as a spirit ever to be re-created and renewed by overcoming routine and refusing to yield to the spirit of institutionalization and "rut." Demo writes:

> The relative attainment of the communitarian spirit normally supposes some preparation, since, after all, not all the members of society at large have the personal detachment required for shared intimacy—for a mutual experience of the reciprocal gift of self, for the acceptance of one's colleagues without selfish restraint.[11]

Christianity, with its values rooted in love, forgiveness, solidarity, the renunciation of oppressive power, the acceptance of others, and so on, is essentially oriented to the creation, within societal structures, of the communitarian spirit.

Meanwhile there is a warning to be heeded. Institutionalization is inevitable in any group that means to last, to be established. With institutionalization comes the codification of successful experiments, and here there can be a threat to community. For its self-preservation, the communitarian spirit has constant need of revitalization. This task will be facilitated if the groups keep relatively small and refuse to allow themselves to be absorbed by institutionality. Here Demo draws an important conclusion for our consideration. *A large organization can be renewed by a community, but it cannot be transformed into a community.*[12] Demo goes even further:

> Therefore all hope vanishes of organizing an entire church along lines of a communitarian network. This would be tantamount to institutionalizing the de-institutionalizing aspect of community. This is not to say that [a community's] formation cannot be organized by well-prepared teams. But its internal experience seems to renew its vitality daily, drinking at its own wells. Indeed, here is its source of strength for protest, here is where it draws its utopian attraction.[13]

In other words the basic church communities, while signifying the communitarian aspect of Christianity, and signifying it within the church, cannot pretend to constitute a global alternative to the church as institution. They can only be its ferment for renewal.

Institutional and Communitarian Elements of the Church in Coexistence

When we say that the basic communities cannot hope to constitute a global alternative to the institutional church, we are not underestimating their genuine value for a renewal of the fabric of the church. We are merely seeking to situate their significance and meaning within the church globally. Without a doubt these communities can be a stimulus for mobilizing new strength in the institutional church, and they represent a call for a more thorough living of the authentically communitarian values of the Christian message. Jesus' whole preaching may be seen as an effort to awaken the strength of these community aspects. In the horizontal dimension Jesus called human beings to mutual respect, generosity, a communion of sisters and brothers, and simplicity in relationships. Vertically he sought to open the human being to a sincere filial relationship with God, to the artlessness of simple prayer, and to generous love for God. Jesus was not much concerned with the institution, apart from demanding that it live in the spirit in which all expressions of human togetherness ought to be lived.

The church in its globalism is the concrete, vital coexistence of the societal, institutional dimension with the communitarian dimension. In the church is an organizing element that transcends particular communities and procures the communion of them all. There is an authority here that symbolizes oneness in love and hope. There is a creed that expresses a basic oneness in faith. There are global goals common to all local communities. Sociological reflection within this church acquires relevance for theology by dispelling illusions, and so helping to keep the correlatives of institution and charism on realistic foundations. Old historical and ecclesiological errors can infiltrate under new names—like too much insistence on a polarization of "traditional church" and "evangelical church," church of the foundation and church of the steeple, ecclesiogenesis and ecclesiology. There can be a genuine renewal of the institutional framework of the church, springing from the impulses of the grassroots communities, without the church losing its identity or being distorted in its historical essence. *The church sprung from the people is the same as the church sprung from the apostles.* What is different is its sociological physiognomy in the world, its forms of liturgical, canonical, and organizational expression. There is no change in the ongoing coexistence of one aspect that is more static, institutional, and permanent with another that is more dynamic, charismatic, and vital. The will to impregnate the institutional, organizational aspect of the church with the spirit of community will never die in the church, and this is the wellspring of its vitality.

After all, the problem of church does not reside in the counterpoint of institution and community. These poles abide forever. *The real problem resides in the manner in which both are lived, the one as well as the other:* whether one pole seeks to absorb the other, cripple it, liquidate it, or each respects the other and opens itself to the other in constant willingness to be put to the question. The latter attitude will not permit the institutional to become necrophiliac and predominate. Nor will it permit the communitarian to degenerate into pure utopianism, which seeks to transform the global church into community. In the church the institutional may not be allowed to predominate over the communitarian. The latter must ever preserve its primacy. The former lives in function of the latter. The communitarian, for its part, must always seek adequate institutional expression.

In the dynamic wave of postconciliar renewal and post-Medellín liberation, two ecclesiological models have emerged in neat distinction. One is oriented to the church as grand institution, with all its services institutionally organized and oriented to the needs of the church universal, the dioceses, and the parishes. This model of the church generally finds its sociological and cultural center in society's affluent sectors, where it enjoys social power and constitutes the church's exclusive interlocutor with the powers of society. The other is centered in the network of the basic communities, deep within the popular sectors and the poor masses, on the margin of power and influence over the media, living the horizontal relationships of coresponsibility and a communion of brothers and sisters more deeply.

Developments in recent years have shown that the church as great institution can no more exist in and for itself, refusing to lend universality to the basic communities and providing them with a linkage with the past, than the network of communities can prescind from the church as great institution. More and more the institution is discovering its meaning and responsibility in the creation, support, and nurture of the communities. To be sure, this has led to a weakening in institutional commitment to the influential sectors of society and state, coupled with a strengthening of evangelical purity and prophecy. For their part, the communities have come more and more to understand their need of the church as great institution, for the maintenance of their continuity, for their Catholic identity, and for their oneness with one another. The convergence of these two ecclesiological models, and their dialectical interaction, has contributed to a profound conscientization of the church as a whole with regard to its missionary activity, especially among the poor of this world, in whose passion it assists and shares. For the church as great institution, the crucial option is becoming daily more difficult to escape: either continue good relations with the state and the wealthy classes represented by the state or take the network of basic communities seriously, with the call for justice and social transformation that this will imply. With the first option, the church as great institution will have its personal and institutional security guaranteed, and will have reliable support for its assisting aid. But it will have to renounce the possibility of efficaciously evangelizing the great masses of the poor. With the second option, the church will recover its prophetic mission, and will carry to the throne of God the cries for justice that rise up from the bowels of the earth. With this option comes also insecurity, official displeasure, and the fate of disciples of Jesus.

What lies in store for the basic community? This, we recall, is the question we asked above. In view of the data we have assembled, we believe we can answer: the basic community has a permanent future, provided it can understand itself in counterpoint to the church as institution. It dare not seek the utopian impossible, and delude itself into believing that it can exhaust the concept of community in its own being, in such wise that no other group or formation could exist. It dare not present itself as the only way of being church today. As we shall see, the basic community constitutes instead a bountiful wellspring of renewal for the tissues of the body ecclesial, and a call and a demand for the evangelical authenticity of ecclesial institutions, so that they may come more closely to approximate the utopian community ideal.

The church never lost this authenticity. It may have lain hidden, like live coals covered with ashes, but today it is emerging in a way never before seen: a rejuvenating leaven of the gospel ideals of communion, in a community of sisters and brothers simply living one and the same faith in the spontaneous worship of Christ in the midst of humanity, and in disinterested service of and concern for the needs of each member. The utopia of the kingdom anticipated in the community of the faithful, a community of more human ties, more lively faith, and more profound communion of members, never died in the church. The basic church community, if it hopes to keep the communitarian spirit alive, may not allow itself to replace the parish. It will have to remain small in order to avoid bureaucratization and to maintain a direct personal relationship among all its members. Although it will have to open up to the communion of the church universal, with all the latter's societal institutions and forms, yet it will have to maintain a dialectical tension with this global church in order not to be absorbed by it. In this way it will deteriorate neither into a fanatical group of futurists nor into a reactionary group in love with the past. Instead it will continue as the abiding leaven of the whole church.

2

Church, or Merely Ecclesial Elements?

Before actually broaching the question in this chapter title, it will be in order to clarify the fundamental characteristic of the basic church community. There are many forms of community. This one is called "church community." By virtue of its "ecclesiality" it is to be distinguished from the others. "Church" here is used as an adjective, modifying the noun "community." And yet in a basic ecclesiological perspective the adjective is more important than the noun, for it is *church* that is the constitutive and structuring principle of this community. The church community is constituted as a response to Christian faith. It comes into being in answer to the gospel call to conversion and salvation. Religious, Christian inspiration welds it together, and assigns it all its objectives, including its social and liberating objectives, which are the earmark of the propagation of the gospel message. Church community means church presence—the living community experience of the gospel, the organism and "organization" of salvation-liberation in the world. It does not mean the cultivation of one or another of human values—athletics, art, music, folk literature, consumer concerns, the defense of human rights. Explicit Christian consciousness constitutes the central trait of this community and is the formal difference between it and other types of community. This Christian consciousness is unquestionable and indispensable.

We have no wish, however, to conceal another problem, typical of certain groups. Some people feel that all authentic community, all community generative of genuine love, self-giving, and mutual assistance, by the mere fact of being genuine community ought to be considered ecclesial, or church, community. Such community does actualize human values. It does concretize the cause of Jesus Christ in history. Therefore, we hear, it is identifiable as church community.

Actually this position is correct, with the following reservation: the theological reality of church—a genuine communion of persons, the conquest of selfishness, the mutual gift of self—is not restricted to the visible limits of church. There is a greater church than the church we see, although it has no awareness of this or any orientation toward a frame of reference of explicit

10

Christian consciousness. No genuinely theological, contemplative world-view, no historico-salvific world-view will ever fail to recognize that grace, salvation, and the activity of the resurrected One are bestowed on the world itself, and not on that part of the world merely that is consciously Christian, the church. This reflection is actually part of the tradition of the church.

The church comes into being as church when people become aware of the call to salvation in Jesus Christ, come together in community, profess the same faith, celebrate the same eschatological liberation, and seek to live the discipleship of Jesus Christ. We can speak of church *in the proper sense* only when there is question of this ecclesial consciousness. Hence the crucial importance of explicit Christian motivation. We are united and we pursue our social objectives of liberation *because* we react to the call of Christ, and the call of other communities that transmit his call to us and that have preceded us in the living experience of this same community faith. We can speak of a *church* community, therefore, only when a given community has this explicit religious and Christian character. Otherwise it will be some other kind of community, however it may actualize the same values as the church pursues. For an authentic, contemplative Christian, this other community indeed verifies the essential definition of church in its ontic reality. But the presence of the ontic ecclesial reality is not enough. In order formally to be church, the *consciousness* of this reality must be there, the profession of explicit faith in Jesus Christ who died and was raised again.

Having clarified this point, we are now in a position to move on to the next—once more, one of special importance.

Differing Opinions

We speak of "basic church communities." Are these communities themselves actually church, or do they merely contain elements of church?

Many different answers are proposed to this question, but this scarcely deprives it of its importance either for ecclesiology or for the actual members of the basic communities. Opinions tend to vary with the position their subjects occupy in the church structure, or with the model of church they adopt as key to the interpretation of total church reality. Thus those within the actual basic communities will tend to consider these communities as church, while those whose orientation is toward the historically established churches will reserve the minimum requirement for church to the parish community. The hierarchy, as we see from Vatican Council II, will define "a church" in terms of diocesan reality, with bishop and Eucharist. Let us consider each of these opinions in turn, and attempt to establish the theological value of each.

First, we shall examine what the basic church community itself says. There is a study carried out by the Centro de Estatística Religiosa e Investigações Sociais (CERIS), in which Father Alfonso Gregory catalogues various responses to the question of the ecclesiality of various experiences.[1] When he comes to the basic communities, he records the following reasons explaining why the basic church community is properly denominated "church":

1. "Because it is founded on the common faith, and its objectives bear on a deepening and an increase of this faith, with all that this implies."
2. "Because there is a direct connection with the ecclesiastical framework, a sense of church-of-the-people." Or, as another respondent put it: "Because it feels its oneness with the parish, diocese, and church universal."
3. "Because in religious activities only Catholics participate, while other activities are ecumenical"—that is, socioeconomic activities. Here we may add what another respondent said: "When you consider yourselves a church community, you can't work when your religious motives are different, or opposite."
4. "Because the strictly religious activities are basic, while all the others are as a consequence of accepting God's word." Or again: "Christianity is the activating of integral humanism."
5. "Because we are working at the grassroots for a communion in faith, through humanization."

But Gregory also documents the contrary view:

The basic communities "are not churches (or, as some would say, they are churches only *juxta modum)*, because, though there may be priests and nuns here, these communities are just beginning. In other cases, their activities are oriented consciously and mainly to the social area."

The vast majority of those responsible for these experiments—the respondents in this research project—feel that they are in contact with actual, genuine church, and not just with ecclesial elements or parachurch communities. José Marins, who is in the front line of defense of the basic communities, puts it well in his reformulation of the thinking of the communities:

For us, the basic church community is the church itself, the universal sacrament of salvation, as it continues the mission of Christ—Prophet, Priest, and Pastor. This is what makes it a community of faith, worship, and love. Its mission is explicitly expressed on all levels—the universal, the diocesan, and the local, or basic.[2]

Elsewhere we read that the basic community is genuine church because it has "the same goals" as the universal church: "to lead all men and women to the full communion of life with the Father and one another, through Jesus Christ, in the gift of the Holy Spirit, by means of the mediating activity of the church."[3] These few citations are representative of the thinking of the great majority of pastoral leaders and theologians directly involved with the basic communities, particularly in Latin America. Most of them consider that the basic church communities constitute the true and authentic presence of the Catholic Church.

Once upon a time the populations in the interior of the Latin American countries, cut off by thick rain forests or other wild territory and scattered over the vast expanses of these empty lands, met together only when the priest came to them—once a year, perhaps, or every six months. Only for this brief moment did they feel themselves to be living church united by the word, together with their ordained minister, around the same altar, celebrating and offering the same sacred Victim. Then came the basic communities, and these same people began to meet every week—or twice a week or every day—to celebrate the presence of the risen One and of his Spirit, to hear and meditate on his word, and to renew their commitment to liberation, together with their community leaders who are the principle of unity and communion with other basic communities and with the parish and diocesan community. Are we now going to tell these people that they are not church, that they have certain "ecclesial elements," but that these do not actually constitute the essence of church?

We must ask ourselves: Are they not baptized? Do they not possess the same faith as the church universal? The same love? The same hope? Do they not read the same Scriptures? Do they not live the same Christian práxis? Are they not fully united to Christ, and are they not the body of Christ? We are not dealing with some mere point of sentimentality here. Let us face the actual ecclesiological problem, and face it objectively. If we are to develop a new ecclesiology, we shall need more than just theological perspicacity and historico-dogmatic erudition. We must face the new experiences of church in our midst. We in Brazil and Latin America are confronted with a new concretization of church, without the presence of consecrated ministers and without the eucharistic celebration. It is not that this absence is not felt, is not painful. It is, rather, that these ministers do not exist in sufficient numbers. This historical situation does not cause the church to disappear. The church abides in the people of God as they continue to come together, convoked by the word and discipleship of Jesus Christ. Something *is* new under the sun: a new church of Christ.

As a result, even those theologians who restrict the definition of church to a community presenting constitutive, essential elements of church such as word, sacrament, the presence of the bishop, and communion with all the other churches—and who therefore pronounce the basic community "not fully church"—are forced nonetheless to conclude: "From the pastoral viewpoint, these basic groups or communities must be considered authentic ecclesial reality—needing development, doubtless, but surely integrated into the one communion of the Father, in Christ, through the Holy Spirit."[4]

The theological problem of the ecclesial character of the basic community must be seen within a context of the recovery by these communities of a true ecclesiological dimension. This is the process now under way in many places. We know that the ninth century saw the rise of papal supremacy. The absolutist ideology of the Gregorian reform two centuries later served to reinforce this development. Then came conciliarism, Gallicanism, and episcopalism, with the attendant polemics. Finally, with the development of the ultramontane ecclesiology and its triumph under Pius IX, the church acquired a unitarian organization, as if it were one great, worldwide diocese, with one sole liturgy, one visible head, one embodiment. Commenting on this, Louis Billot writes:

> The ultimate result of this development in modern theology has been a genuine ignorance of the ecclesial quality of the local churches [the dioceses]. These would be thought of as "imperfect societies," lacking the necessary means for the realization of their end, which is the eternal salvation of the human being.[5]

Vatican II transcended this state of affairs, recognizing the local or particular church as genuine church, but without developing a complete theology of the local church. An important step has been taken, then, in the process of defining what it is to be a particular or local church, and restoring to it its proper evaluation. Vatican II defined the particular church as

> that portion of God's people which is entrusted to a bishop to be shepherded by him with the cooperation of the presbytery. Adhering thus to its pastor and gathered together by him in the Holy Spirit through the gospel and the Eucharist, this portion constitutes a particular church in which the one, holy, catholic, and apostolic church of Christ is truly present and operative.[6]

The particular church, then, is defined in diocesan terms. Unity is secured through the presence of the bishop and the celebration of the Eucharist. The capacity to represent the church universal is not, however, reserved to the diocese gathered around the bishop in the celebration of the Eucharist. *Lumen Gentium* says:

> This church of Christ is truly present in all legitimate local congregations of the faithful . . . united with their pastors . . . . In them the faithful are gathered together by the preaching of the gospel of Christ, and the mystery of the Lord's Supper is celebrated, "that by the flesh and blood of the Lord's body the whole brotherhood may be joined together [citing "Mozarabic prayer: *PL* 96, 759B"].
>   . . . In these communities, though frequently small and poor, or living far from any other, Christ is present. By virtue of Him the one, holy, catholic, and apostolic Church gathers together.[7]

In all cases, then, the essential constitutive element of a particular church as church, for Vatican Council II, is always the gospel, the Eucharist, and the presence of the apostolic succession in the person of the bishop.[8]

Medellín, in 1968, could already testify to an evolution in the ecclesial experience of the postconciliar era, with the rise of basic communities all over the South American continent:

Thus the Christian base community is *the first and fundamental ecclesiastical nucleus*, which on its own level must make itself responsible for the richness and expansion of the faith, as well as of the cult which is its expression. This community becomes then the *initial cell* of the ecclesiastical structures and the focus of evangelization, and it currently serves as the most important source of human advancement and development. The essential element for the existence of Christian base communities are their leaders or directors. These can be priests, deacons, men or women religious, or laymen [italics added].[9]

There is no mention here of the elements of bishop and Eucharist. The church is not being thought of from the top down, but from the bottom up, from the grassroots, from the "base." The church—"God's family"—takes form by "means of a nucleus, although it be small, which creates a community of faith, hope and charity."[10] Truly another step has been taken in a grasp of the church dimension of the basic communities.

This new reflection on new ecclesial actualities at the grassroots of the church did not fail to have its repercussions on the 1974 Synod of Bishops. The French-speaking Group B—comprising patriarchs and bishops of the Eastern churches, bishops of the traditional churches of Europe, and bishops of the young churches of Asia and Africa—through their reporters, Father Lecuyer and Bishop Matagrin, proposed a broader definition for "local church":

It seems better, for pastoral reasons, not to reserve the expression "particular church" to a diocese (cf. *Lumen Gentium*, nos. 23, 27), but, rather, to use it to designate any church rendering the service of the gospel in a particular human community, in communion with all the particular churches, which constitute the church universal.[11]

This broader concept will have a direct bearing on the problem of the nature of the basic communities as genuine church. We shall now attempt to offer a fundamental ecclesiological reflection, with a view to a more adequate understanding of the ecclesial nature of the basic church communities. We shall make use of a key category of the ecclesiology of Vatican II—the church as universal sacrament of salvation—attempting to link this concept with the broader problematic of the relationship of the particular church to the universal church.

Routes to a Broader Understanding of the Ecclesiality of the Basic Communities: A Reflection

We do not presume to enter upon a terminological discussion of "local church" versus "particular church" or "Catholic Church" versus "universal church." Cardinal Baggio thought "particular church" should be restricted to dioceses, and "local church" used for infradiocesan communities—parishes, basic communities, religious communities.[12] Henri de Lubac gives these terms a different set of meanings: the extent of a local church will be determined by criteria of a sociocultural order.[13] A local church will be composed of various particular churches, gathered together in one geographical, social, and cultural space, while a particular church will be a diocese—what *Lumen Gentium* calls a "communitas altaris sub episcopi sacro ministerio" ("community existing around an altar, under the sacred ministry of the bishop"[14]). The "particular church," then, will be defined by essentially theological criteria.[15]

Somewhat analogously, de Lubac distinguishes between "universal church" and "Catholic Church." The former term would have a stronger connotation of quantitative or geographical extension ("Ecclesia per totum orbem terrarum diffusa"); the latter would suggest qualitative nondispersion—orientation toward a center that would guarantee unity regardless of spatial extension or internal differentiation. Catholicity is a quality of any given particular church in virtue of the communion of this church with the other churches.[16]

Vatican II made none of these distinctions, using the terms of each pair indifferently. And indeed, what is important is not the words but their correct theological understanding. And so we leave this terminological question open.

Universal versus Particular

A serious hermeneutical problem, however, lurks behind the terminological distinction of universal and particular. The question of the one and the many is not a specifically ecclesiological problem, of course, but a basic one for all thought, and it has been one of the keys to philosophy from the days of the ancient Greeks onward. Reflection on this problem in ecclesiology seems insufficient. Textual citation and factual observation are simply used instead. For example, one of the facts observed is that the New Testament makes two sorts of propositions: (1) The church is one. As there is one God, one Lord, one Spirit, one bread, one baptism, one faith—so also there is one church (cf. Eph. 4:4–6). This church is universal and includes all the faithful regardless of their origin, race, nation, or culture. (2) The church is multiple. It is formed of a multiplicity of communities differentiated by city, province, local conditions, and sociocultural idiosyncracies (cf. 1 Thess. 2:14; 1 Cor. 1:19; 2 Cor. 8:1; Acts 15:41; 16:5; 18:22).

How is the relationship between the one church and the multiple church to be conceived? Or first: What is the one (universal) church and what is the particular (multiple) church? The one, universal church, for Paul, for instance, consists in the mystery of salvation of God, realized by the Son, in the power of the Holy Spirit acting within history and reaching all human beings. This mystery is one because God is one. It is universal because it touches each and every human being.[17] The universality of the church resides in the universality of God's salvific offer. But this universal salvific mystery is manifested in space and time, and in being revealed it takes on the particularities of ages and places. Thus there arises a particular church. This particular church is the universal church, manifested—concretized, historicized. "It is the universal church, happening."[18] As Father Vaz has said so well:

> The universal church is not a *whole*, whose *parts* are the particular churches (quantitatively extrinsic). Nor does it exist after the fashion of a *substance* with the particular churches as its *accidents* (substantively extrinsic). . . . Nor does it exist as a *potential* or virtual whole, with the particular churches as its *actualizations* "here and now" (qualitatively extrinsic. . . . The universal church is in the particular churches whole, and has in them its phenomenal, or reflex, reality. Whatever is attributed to the universal church is attributed to the particular church. . . . We have the universal church, which is intrinsically differentiated, or manifested, in the particularity of the local churches. (Even the Church of Rome is a local church.)[19]

Catholicity, therefore, is not a geographical concept (a church present in all parts of the world). Nor is it a statistical concept (a church quantitatively more numerous). Nor is it a sociological concept (a church inserted into every culture). Nor indeed is it a historical concept (a church preserving its identity through the centuries). To be Catholic, it must preserve its true identity (not just any identity) always and everywhere.[20] And this identity resides in the unity, the singleness, of its faith in God, who has sent the Son in order to save, in the power of the Holy Spirit, all men and women—this faith being mediated by the church, the universal sacrament of salvation.

The universal church therefore possesses the nature of mystery, of divine transcendence, of universality. It is, as the Fathers of the church used to say, *prima novissima*, the first of the last things. It is *ab aeternitate*, from all eternity. It does not exist in the way that things and particular churches exist— limited to one space and one time and to the singularity of each thing's particular manifestations. It exists in the form of mystery, which is the manner of existence of God: above and beyond all limits and determinations whatever. Hence, as Louis Bouyer says: "The one and universal Church does not manifest herself, nor has she any concrete existence, properly speaking, except in the local churches."[21]

What the Particular Church Is Not. The particular church is not a part of some whole supposedly existing in itself in physical form and called the universal church. It is not to be confused with Rome. Rome is a locality and has a local church. (Of course, this local church may well be the church constitituted as the sign of unity of the universal church present in all particular churches.) If a particular church were part of a whole, this would mean the atomization of ecclesial space. The universal church would be the sum of its parts, and thus the result of those parts. Instead, the universal church is always the *prima novissima*, the structuring, originating principle of all.

The particular church is not a local agency of a broader administrative body.

The New Testament never speaks of a particular church as a part of a whole. The image of body and members or of head and members represents the relationship between Christ and the church, not that between the universal church and the local church. The particular church is not a part of a whole, but rather, a portion oriented toward a whole.[22]

The particular church is not formed of particular elements per se, but of elements that are common to all particular churches; by that very fact that these elements are particular elements. Still, what is common is not necessarily universal: the common may be the particular, found everywhere—in the case before us, found in the various particular churches. The universal is that which, in difference and within particular difference, remains the same. In the case of the church, the universal element is God's salvific will.

The particular church is not an element or entity of a confederation. In a confederation, each entity is separately constituted, and only subsequently enters into a relationship, "joins" the whole. If this were the case with the church, the universal church would be a result, a consequence.

What the Particular Church Is. The particular church is the universal church (the salvific will in Christ through the Spirit) in its phenomenal, or sacramental, presentation.

The particular church is the universal church rendered visible within the framework of a time and a place, a medium and a culture.

The particular church is the universal church concretized; and in being concretized, taking flesh; and in taking flesh, assuming the limits of place, time, culture, and human beings.

The particular church is the whole mystery of salvation in Christ—the universal church—in history, but not the totality of the history of the mystery of salvation in Christ. For each particular church is in itself limited and, precisely, particular. Accordingly, each particular church must be open to the others, which likewise, each in its own manner, concretize and manifest the same universal salvific mystery—that is, the church universal.

The particular church is the church wholly, but not the whole church. *It is the church wholly* because in each particular church is contained the whole mystery of salvation. But *it is not the whole church* because no particular church exhausts by itself the whole wealth of the mystery of salvation. That mystery can and must be expressed in other particular churches, and in other particular forms. The identification of the universal church with one particular church (like the Church of Rome) is a moment in the history (and a concretization of the history) of the universal church itself as thus revealed and "historicized" in the triumph of the identical and homogeneous: one language, one liturgy, one code of canon law, one way of doing theology. In this way the universalization of the particular was achieved—the particular of the local Church of Rome. Historically the particular Church of Rome has imposed itself upon all the other particular churches. But the Church of Rome has not ceased for all that to be a particular church. The universal has not become singular and homogenized. The universal is openness to all sides, and, in the case of the church, openness especially to the salvific mystery that is manifested in each particular church. Without this openness and koinonia, the particular church ceases to be church because it ceases to be universal.

The Minimal Constitutive Reality of the Particular Church

We have seen that the church universal—the mystery of salvation, the *ecclesia deorsum*, the church-from-above—enjoys a primacy over the particular churches because it is this church-from-above that exists in them all. How does this church concretely come to be in the midst of men and women?

The particular church is not merely a gift from above, as the universal church is. It is also a (particular) human effort. It is God's salvific offer, and simultaneously human beings' humble acceptance. Faith is the act by which human beings open themselves to God and accept in their lives the salvation, forgiveness, and indwelling of the triune God. In this sense, faith is antecedent to the particular, concrete, institutionalized church.[23] Faith constitutes the initiating and structuring principle of the particular church. The latter is defined most basically as a *communitas fidelium*, a community of those who believe, an assembly of those who gather together by reason of and for the sake of their faith. *Faith, therefore, constitutes the minimum constitutive reality of the particular church.*

Faith is given essentially as communion. Therefore the particular church is also essentially communion. Believing in Jesus Christ the Savior, the particular church is established as communion with him who is seated at the right hand of God and continues to act in the power of the Spirit. Concrete faith is bestowed via those mediations that present Jesus to the world and keep his memory alive down through history. Faith establishes communion with the particular churches that live Jesus' message in the fidelity of the apostolic succession. Faith, then, establishes a vertical communion with God and the risen Jesus Christ, to which corresponds a horizontal communion with those who share the same faith. In Christian faith in Jesus Christ the Savior, whose salvation begins to be realized here and now in the present life, there exists, in seed and germ, the totality of the Christian mystery. There are not many mysteries in Christianity. Basically there is but one great mystery: the mystery of the trinitarian God who communicates to human beings in definitive and eschatological form in Jesus Christ and who continues to communicate through the presence of the Holy Spirit. "Mysteries," in the plural, are specifications of this *mysterium simplicitatis*, to use the expression the martyr Speratus used when arraigned before the consul Saturninus.[24]

These reflections force us to the following conclusion: *believers, by reason of their faith-and-community, are already, in themselves, the presence of the universal church.* True, they express it only to a limited extent, but they do express it. The expression becomes more perceptible when believers gather together in faith, celebrate salvation, and make themselves available for ministering salvation. This visible expression will be still greater when the group of faithful thus gathered together has a leader among them, a symbol of their oneness with one another and with other communities, and when they can celebrate the eucharistic presence of the Lord sacramentally. Finally, this sacramental expression, this visible expression, can grow greater and greater in larger communities, since these have the capacity to render explicit the whole abundance of riches contained in the mystery of salvation, on the social level, the liturgical level, the theological level, the canonical level. All these expressions, different though they be, concretize, each in its own way, one and the same mystery, one and the same universal church.

Saint Paul employs the same expression, "church," for all forms of the church's becoming visible: in a particular *family* (". . . the congregation [*ekklēsia*] that meets in their house," Rom. 16:3–5; cf. 1 Cor. 16:19, Col. 4:15; Philem. 2); in a particular *city* ("the church of God which is in Corinth," 1 Cor. 1:2; cf. 2 Cor. 1:1; Rev. 2:8; 3:7); in a particular *province* (". . . the instructions I gave the churches of Galatia," 1 Cor. 16:1; cf. 16:19; 2 Cor. 8:1); or on the level of the church as scattered throughout *various regions* of the empire (Rom. 16:16, 23; Col. 1:24). The forms of visibility become gradually more explicit, and all alike receive the name of "church." In other words, the universal church, the church of the living God (1 Tim. 3:15), which is the body of Christ (Eph. 1:22) because Christ is its Head (Col. 1:18), is manifested, emerges phenomenologically, comes to concrete realization in the various particular churches in which the faithful gather to express their faith, celebrate the presence of the Spirit, and commune with their fellow Christians. None exhausts the wealth of the salvific mystery, and so each must be open to the others, and all of these to the church of glory, where alone the church will attain to its plenitude. No particular church (no diocesan church, Roman or any other, however illustrious its apostolic tradition, its liturgy, and its saints and doctors) may close in upon itself or impose itself upon others and constrain them to accept its particularities. The particular church must be open not only to its counterparts, but to the eschatological church as well. The particular church is *in via*, is still imperfect, incomplete, holy and penitent, for it is sinful. It will be complete, fulfilled, when the Lord comes at the last.

Taking these reflections as consistent and conclusive, we may say that the basic church communities, in all theological rigor, are true, universal church, concretized on this small-group level. The basic community (as described in the seminar held in Maringá, Brazil, from May 1 to 3, 1972, which dealt with these communities) is "a group, or complex of groups, of persons in which a primary, personal relationship of brotherly and sisterly communion obtains, and which lives the totality of the life of the church, as expressed in service, celebration, and evangelization."[25]

Sacrament: Unity of Universal and Particular

How may one express concisely the oneness obtaining between the church universal and the particular churches? Tradition has found a category for this,

Vatican II has made it official, and theology has propagated it: the church is the universal sacrament of unity and salvation. *Sacramentum* is a Latin translation of the Greek word *mustērion, mysterium*. Mystery, or sacrament, as applied to the church, said the council of fathers in working out their draft of the Constitution on the Church in the Modern World, does not mean something abstruse, but—and many theologians stress this today—a transcendent, salvific reality, which manifests itself in its own particular visible way. The official document says:

> Christ . . . established and ceaselessly sustains here on earth His holy Church . . . as a visible structure. . . . But [this] society . . . and the Mystical Body of Christ are not to be considered as two realities. . . . Rather they form one interlocked reality which is comprised of a divine and a human element. For this reason, by an excellent analogy, this reality is compared to the mystery of the incarnate Word. Just as the assumed nature inseparably united to the divine Word serves Him as a living instrument of salvation, so, in a similar way, does the communal structure of the Church serve Christ's Spirit, who vivifies it by way of building up the body [cf. Eph. 4:16].[26]

The concept of sacrament or mystery, then, expresses precisely the oneness of the universal church with the particular churches: it is always the universal church—the mystery of salvation, God's salvific design—which is manifested in the differences occurring in human beings' history.

Grace and salvation are always expressed in sacramental form. They do not come like a bolt from the blue. They find their path to hearts of human beings through all manner of mediations. The mediations can change, but grace and faith cannot. ("Mutata sunt sacramenta, sed non fides," Saint Augustine never tired of repeating.) When Vatican Council II speaks of the church as the "universal sacrament of salvation," it is thinking in historico-salvific terms: the interior reality of the visible, historical church—the particular churches—reaches out beyond these churches, in the mystery of the church universal, to touch all human beings visibly, from the just Abel to the last of the elect.[27] This visibility varies in form and can take on the most diverse condensations. It begins in the atheist of goodwill, in his or her quest for goodness and truth.[28] It gains further visibility in the nonevangelized, in their religious life.[29] It takes on still further density in Jews and other unbaptized monotheists.[30] It wins the name of "church" among baptized Christians, even those not living within the Roman Catholic Church.[31] It appears in all its sacramental, visible richness in the apostolic Roman Church.[32] And it attains to its fullness in the church of glory.[33] It is this entire reality that makes up the "sacrament of unity."[34] The church is not a composed reality, then, but a "complex" one, as the Vatican Council states.[35] Preserving their oneness all the while, the visible elements may vary. Variation does not destroy communion.[36]

If the church as sacrament knows various sorts of concretizations even beyond the confines of the Roman Catholic Church, so much the more will it find them within itself. Thus we can say that the basic church community truly constitutes church-as-sacrament. The universal church historicizes salvation, becomes its sign and instrument, wherever and however it takes root in a culture. The basic community represents a particular type of sacramentality, of visibility; but in this concrete visibility, open to development and to the manifestation of much more than it presently manifests of the mystery hidden within it, the whole universal church is to be found.

The church-as-sacrament is a mystery of communion, of God with human beings and of human beings among themselves. Where there is communion with God, we know that there is communion with others (cf. 1 Jn. 3:6–7). This communion can be expressed in many symbols or few. It can take different forms of visibility. But it must be present in the churches. Without it they would not be churches. *Therefore communion is an indivisible reality, not admitting of degree. Communion either is present or is not present.* Communion among all the churches is expressed by symbols that translate and reinforce this union. The heads of local churches, besides constituting a principle of internal unity, constitute as well a principle of oneness with the other churches: the head of the basic community, the pastor of the parish, the bishop of the diocese, the pope of the whole church. A single creed, the same basic structures of liturgy, of juridical ordination, of theological understanding form instances of the expression of the unity, the oneness, of all the churches. These instances do not constitute the universal church. The latter exists only in the local churches, which, via these persons and instances, articulate their communion with one another and with the triune God.[37]

At Pentecost the Spirit descended upon all present and caused each one to hear the same message, albeit in a diversity of languages. It did not make all speak the same language. It made all hear the same message.[38] This is a prefiguring of the "one . . . Catholic . . . Church"—a prefiguring of the oneness and catholicity of the church, with one and the same universal church being concretized in multiple particular churches. The church's destiny in the world is to grow until it can speak every language under heaven in order to express one and the same experience of the salvation that comes from God through the Son Jesus Christ in the power of the Holy Spirit. In their own particular way, the basic ecclesial communities incarnate this experience of salvation. Therefore they are indeed authentic universal church become reality at the grassroots.

3

The Reinvention of the Church

Ways of Being Church

The rise of the basic church communities and the praxis of these communities are of matchless value when it comes to questioning the prevailing manner of being church. They are sprung from basic, minimum elements like faith, the reading of the word and meditation on it, and mutual assistance in all human dimensions. As we have seen, they are genuine church. Many functions, genuinely new ministries, appear in them—ministries of community coordination, of catechesis, of organizing the liturgy, of caring for the sick, of teaching people to read and write, of looking after the poor, and the like. All this is done in a deep spirit of communion, with a sense of joint responsibility and with an awareness of building and living actual church. The best conceptualization of this experience is in the frequently heard expression, "reinvention of the church." The church is beginning to be born at the grassroots, beginning to be born at the heart of God's People. This experience calls into question the common fashion of considering oneself to be church. It enables one to discover the true source of the ongoing birth and creation of the church: the Holy Spirit.

The church can be considered from many points of view. Indeed there are as many ecclesiologies as there are basic ecclesial structures. There are those who work out their understanding of church from its priestly-episcopal-papal structure, although this yields not so much an ecclesiology as a "parochiology." There are those whose thinking begins with the word/sacrament structure, so that we have preeminently a prophetico-cultic picture of church. There are those who articulate the church from the figure of the church on a journey, and then we get a preeminently historico-salvific vision. And there are more. All these ecclesiologies have their sense, their meaning. But each is limited in itself, and must be opened out upon other forms of theoretical totalization of the mystery of church. Otherwise we have an oppressive ideologization of categories against categories, and the faith community suffers harm.

The basic church communities are aiding the whole church to overcome an internal obstacle under which it has labored for centuries, and which has

23

prevented it from seeing the more abundant riches of the mystery of church. The church, in the Latin West, has been thought of in terms of a Christ/church polarity, within a juridical vision. The relationships between Christ and the church are formulated on the model of the relationships of a society with its founder. Christ transmits all power to the Twelve, who transmit it to their successors, the bishops and the pope. The latter have been considered as the sole depositaries of all responsibility, and have been seen as amassing for themselves all power in the church, in such wise that they are pictured as in confrontation with the community. Thus the actual community is divided between rulers and governed, between celebrants and onlookers, between producers and consumers of sacraments. In a like systematization, the hierarchy constitutes the sole representative of the universal church and the particular church.

This image suppresses the other one—that of the church as faith community *(communitas fidelium),* globally coresponsible for all the affairs of the church. Further, one begins with the shepherds who are responsible for the flock. But this is to invert the natural order: first comes the flock, and then, for the sake of the flock, the shepherd. *The hierarchical function is essential in the church—but it does not subsist in and for itself.* The hierarchical function must be understood—this is the simple and natural understanding of things—as subsisting within the faith community and in its service, whether by representing all the other churches vis-à-vis this particular church (the authentic face-to-face dimension of any community-and-head), or as principle of unity at the heart of the local church, of which the head is actually a member. The other understanding of church, furthermore, is predicated on a particular Christology which permits it to take Christ only in his sarkical, or fleshly, existence; it does not consider the risen Christ, with the transformations that his resurrection has conferred upon him: his cosmic ubiquity, the spiritual nature of his body *(sōma pneumatikon,* 1 Cor. 15:44), and so on. This consideration would render the institution of the church more flexible, and would reintroduce the "pneumatic" element as part and parcel of the Christological element. *The church was born not only from the opened side of Christ, but from the Holy Spirit, as well, on the day of Pentecost.* The unity between these two elements is found in Jesus Christ who died and was raised again as the maximum presence of the Holy Spirit in the world, in such wise that we can say: Jesus-according-to-the-flesh constituted the greatest presence of the Holy Spirit in the world; and the Holy Spirit in the church is now the presence-in-history of the risen Christ.[1]

The basic church communities help the whole church to consider itself from the viewpoint of a reality that is more basic, and without which the church does not exist. That reality is faith in the active presence of the risen One and of his Spirit at the heart of every human community, efficaciously enabling it both to live the essential values, without which there is no humanity, and to open out to the Absolute, without whom there is no dignity or salvation. This divine activity acquires a special density in the church. But it excludes no human person. This contemplative view modifies the manner of being church. Now the clergy moves into the midst of the people, toward persons already activated by the Spirit, which, before the arrival of the institutional church, was already shaping an anonymous church by its grace, its forgiveness. This is not a matter, then, of *transplanting* the church deductively, but of *implanting* the church inductively. As Cardinal Darmojuwono, president of the Indonesian Bishops Conference, said in the Synod of 1974: "To implant the church is to enter into dialogue with the culture and the religions of the country. The object of this dialogue is to render gradually more explicit and conscious the presence of God's Spirit, which transforms and penetrates human beings' lives."[2]

The church that is implanted explicates, purifies, and prolongs the already existing, latent church. The basic church communities are born of this Spirit manifested and organized in the midst of the People of God. The recognition of the presence of the risen One and of the Spirit in the hearts of human beings leads one to conceptualize the church more from the foundation up than from the steeple down. It means accepting the coresponsibility of all in the upbuilding of the church, not just of a limited number belonging to the clerical institution.

We might represent these two conceptualizations of church in the following schemata:

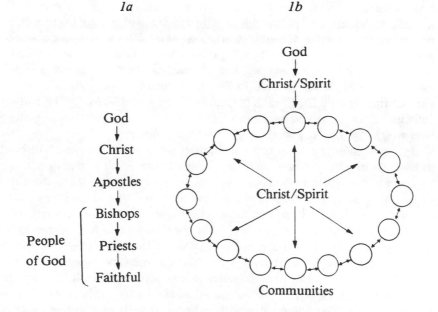

Figure 1, a and b. Conceptualizations of Church.

In Fig. 1a the category "People of God" arises as the result of a previous organization. The power in this organization is concentrated along the axis of bishop/priest. The laity only receive. They do not produce in terms of organization or structure, but only in terms of reinforcement of the structure. One wonders: Is it really the organization that creates the church? Or does the organization arise, as second act, because the community that is the People of God exists antecedently, as first act? It seems to us that the latter conceptualization is the authentic one. The former would be the ideology of the dominant class, calculated to safeguard the rights and prerogatives of that class. Further, this ecclesiological conception is governed by the category of "power." According to this conception, Christ and the Spirit possess no direct immanence. Their only immanence is mediated by the ordained ministry. Hence it is the hierarchy that occupies the center of interest, rather than the risen One, and the Spirit with its charisms. Christ and the Spirit begin, as it were, on the outside, and are brought into the community by means of the representative and sacramental function of the hierarchy. The Christ-Spirit-Church relation is presented not as a vital fabric, an interwoven tissue, but in an exteriority, after the fashion of the relationship of an institution with its founder. This conceptualization is less theological than juridical. The power in question is divine only in its origin. In its exercise it follows the mechanisms of any profane power with its mechanisms of coercion, security, and control.

In Fig. 1b the reality that is God's People emerges as primary instance; its organization is seen as secondary, derived, and at the service of the primary. Christ's power (*exousia*) resides not only in certain members, but in the totality of the People of God as vehicle of Christ's triple ministry of witness, oneness, and worship. This power of Christ's is diversified in accordance with specific functions, but it leaves no one out. The laity emerge as creators of ecclesiological values. In this sense Vatican II's Decree on the Missionary Activity of the Church rings true: "The Church has not been truly established, and is not yet fully alive, nor is it a perfect sign of Christ among men, unless there exists a laity worthy of the name working along with the hierarchy."[3]

Before becoming visible through human mediations—those of bishop, priest, deacon, and so on—the risen Christ and the Spirit already possess a presence in the community. There prevails an ongoing, constant immanence of the Spirit and of the risen Lord in humanity, and in a special way in the community of the faithful. It is these who gather to form the church, who constitute it essentially. *The hierarchy has the sacramental function of organizing and serving a reality that it has not created but discovered, and within which it finds itself.* The theologico-mystical element always has primacy over the juridical. In this understanding it is no longer difficult to grasp the ecclesiality of the basic church communities, and to assign theological value to the various services which arise within the community as manifestations of the Spirit.

As our reflections have shown, the problem of ministries is linked to the model of church on which it is predicated. This model must be submitted to analysis and critique. The basic communities concretize a conception of church as a communion of sisters and brothers, as church-community, church-body-of-Christ, church-People-of-God.

In a *first moment*, a basic equality of all persons is assumed. By faith and baptism all are directly grafted onto Christ. The Spirit becomes present in all, creating a community and a genuine communion of persons, where differences of sex, nation, intelligence, and social position are of no account, since "all are one in Christ Jesus" (Gal. 3:28). In this community all are sent, not just some; all are responsible for the church, not just a few; all must bear prophetic witness, not just a few persons; all must sanctify, not just some.

In a *second moment*, differences and hierarchy arise within the unity of, and in function of, the community. All are equal, but not all do everything. A great number of needs appear, and these have to be attended to. There are different tasks, functions, and services (cf. Rom. 12; 1 Cor. 12). As Vatican II puts it so well:

> Not only . . . is the People of God made up of different peoples but even in its inner structure it is composed of various ranks. This diversity among its members arises either by reason of their duties, as is the case with those who exercise the sacred ministry for the good of their brethren, or by reason of their situation and way of life, as is the case with those many who enter the religious state and, tending toward holiness by a narrower path, stimulate their brethren by their example.[4]

In Pauline language, the church-body-of-the-Lord is said to own manifold charisms. The concept of charism is not restricted to extraordinary manifestations of the Spirit. It is concretized in the ordinary everyday, as in love, which is the most excellent of charisms (1 Cor. 12:37). Every baptized member of the community is charismatic, since each has his or her place and function: "Each one has his own gift from God, one this and another that" (1 Cor. 7:7). "To each person the manifestation of the Spirit is given for the common good" (1 Cor. 12:7; cf. 1 Pet. 4:10). No one is useless or idle. We are "individually members one of another. We have gifts that differ," and these gifts "should be used for service" (Rom. 12:5, 7), so that each member may ever be at the disposition of the others.

Charism, therefore, may be understood as each person's own function in the community as a form of manifestation of the Spirit within the community for the community's good. Charism, as Hans Küng defines it, is "God's call to the individual person in view of a specific service within the community, including the ability to perform this service."[5] Or, as another leading specialist in the area, Gotthold Hasenhüttl, defines it: "Charism is the concrete call, received through the salvific event, exercised in the community, constituting that community in ongoing fashion, building it, and serving human beings in love."[6] Charism, in this sense, is not something incidental and adventitious to church, something that could be wanting to it. It is actually constitutive of church-as-community. Community always appears as organized, however true it be that that organization occurs within the community and is a subdetermination of the community itself—which is antecedent to the organization.

Now we can say that Jesus did not select the Twelve as founders of future churches. *Jesus established the Twelve as a community: as messianic, eschato-logical church.* The apostles are not to be understood first and foremost as individuals, but precisely as the *Twelve*, as messianic community gathered around Jesus and his Spirit. This community then broadened and gave rise to other apostolic communities.

This conceptualization of the church as a community of faith, with a variety of functions, services, and tasks, at once occasions a problem. Who will see to the unity of the whole, to the order and harmony of all the charisms, in such wise that all things will work together for the upbuilding of the same body? Here, then, is the need for a specific charism, that of the principle of unity among all the charisms. This will be the charism of assistance, of direction, of administration (cf. 1 Cor. 12:28), the charism of those who preside over and see to the oneness of the whole (1 Thess. 5:12; Rom. 12:8; 1 Tim. 5:17). *The specific formality of this charism does not reside in accumulation and absorp-tion, but in integration and coordination.* This charism is not outside the community, but within it; not over the community, but for the good of the community. The "monitor" in a basic community, the pastor in a parish, the bishop in a diocese, the pope in the church—all are principles of oneness within a particular local church and, beyond this church, with all the other churches. The service of unity, from monitor to pope, is not an autocratic power *over* the church, but a power at its heart and for its service. As Saint Augustine put it, "I am a bishop for you, and a Christian with you." There is no such thing as absolute ordination to the function of direction. There is no such thing as a monitor without a community, a pastor without a parish, a bishop without a diocese. The councils of Nicea (325) and Chalcedon (451) therefore consider absolute ordinations null.[7] And today bishops without an actual diocese must have a "titular see," a "defunct see" somewhere in the world, so that they, too, may be bishops of a particular church, and not just a new sort of *episcopi vagantes.*

In order to construct this unity, the one presiding in the community is endowed with a special grace. The oneness of the church is not immanent grandeur, but theological grandeur: it is oneness with the various churches, including the Church of Rome, which "presides over all in charity," as Saint Ignatius of Antioch wrote at the turn of the first century, and it is oneness with the church universal. The nature of the ministry of unity as service therefore implies an ontological character (in the form of a special grace) that is abiding, that is ongoing, for it looks to a permanent need of the commu-nity.

We may diagram this model of the church as community of services as follows.

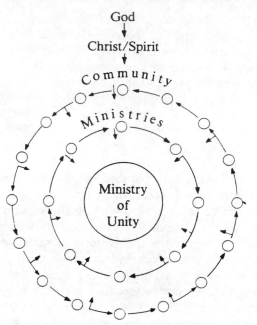

Figure 2. The Church as Community of Services.

In Fig. 2 (despite all the risks of diagrams) it clearly appears how all services arise within the community and for the community. This diagram is a concrete representation of how basic church communities function, and how
they can serve in the recovery of a more evangelical sense of church for our
days: for this model corresponds better to the ideals preached and lived by
Jesus Christ. The New Testament, of course, offers several models of
church. One—in Matthew—is more pyramidal, though with a strong accent
on fellowship and communion. Another—in Paul's letters—is more circular,
more communitarian-and-charismatic. Another—that of the Catholic epis-
tles—is more explicitly oriented along the lines of the permanent functions of
presbyters and bishops. What Jesus had in mind with the Twelve was not just
hierarchy but church, for it was from among the community of the disciples
that he chose the Twelve. We endorse Yves Congar's statement:

> Jesus instituted a structured community, a community in its entirety holy,
> priestly, prophetic, missionary, and apostolic, with ministries at its interior:
> some freely aroused by the Spirit, others bound by the imposition of hands
> to the institution and mission of the Twelve. A linear diagram, then, must be
> replaced by one in which the community appears as the all-embracing reality
> within which the ministries, even those that are instituted and sacramental,
> take their position as services of precisely what the community is called to be
> and to do.[8]

This problem raises another. What sort of organization did Jesus want for his church? Here a great diversity of opinion reigns in Catholic and ecumenical theology today. We shall attempt to come to grips with it briefly later in this book. The Acts of the Apostles (6:1–6) suggests that the church created the ministries of which it had need, within the framework of its essential apostolicity. Basically, the community must be outfitted with "roles of service" (Eph. 4:12)—with those services, structures, and functions that become necessary in order to render present the risen One, his message, and his Spirit among human persons in such wise as he may be a God-spel, Good News, for them, especially for the poor.

The existence and the functioning of the basic church communities permits us to construct, in simpler and more realistic terms, a whole new state of the question of ministries as subdeterminations of a living and vital model of church: the model of church-community-of-sisters-and-brothers; the model of sacrament of integral liberation in the world, a sacrament endowed with a multitude of charisms. A theological reading enables us to accept as genuine ministries the various services that are rendered in community, some of them permanent and seeing to permanent needs, others transitory and bound up with persons having some special charism. Various services take on different forms as the Spirit becomes present and operative in the community.[9]

Growing beyond Current Church Structure

The form in which the basic church communities are organized, and the praxis that develops within them, can make a mighty contribution when it comes to overcoming a fundamental obstacle to communitarian life: the current structure of participation in the church. The church is structured, rather, in a schematic and rigid form, as diagrammed in Fig. 3:[10]

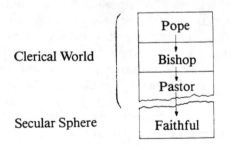

Figure 3. Traditional Church Structure.

In terms of decision, the participation of the faithful is totally mutilated. Decision is restricted to the pope-bishop-pastor axis. A community in which the routes of participation are cut off in all directions cannot pretend to the name of community. In a community, as we have stressed, equality must prevail in conjunction with a face-to-face communion of members. And there is a

further, aggravating factor: this linear structure has been dogmatically repro-
duced and consecrated. It has been socialized by theology, and internalized by
the ministers themselves, who, in striking their mutual relationships, do so in
the framework of the prevailing structure, and thus perpetuate the problem. In
this type of relationship the bishop, for example, does not enter into direct
contact with the faithful, but only with the priest. As *Lumen Gentium* expressly says:

> Associated with their bishop in a spirit of trust and generosity, priests make
> him present in a certain sense in the individual local congregations of the
> faithful, and take upon themselves, as far as they are able, his duties and
> concerns, discharging them with daily care. As they sanctify and govern
> under the bishop's authority that part of the Lord's flock entrusted to them,
> they make the universal Church visible in their own locality and lend
> powerful assistance to the upbuilding of the whole body of Christ (cf. Eph.
> 4:12).[11]

Carlos Alberto de Medina and Pedro A. Ribeira de Oliveira, sociologists of
the Centro de Estatística Religiosa e Investigações Sociais (CERIS), have
analyzed most incisively and with great perception the functioning of this
linear, descending line in the Church of Brazil.[12] (Their analysis is valid for the
whole church, however, for the church in Brazil reproduces the system uni-
formly and universally prevailing there.) They find that in the Brazilian church
the roles of each agent are defined in such a way that the faithful, in terms of
participation in decisions, are excluded. The faithful are not the vehicles of
decision-making ecclesial reality. The framework of the church may undergo
renovation, the laity may be given a share in ecclesial and ecclesiastical activities, but, thanks to the power structure in the church, the damper is put on
when it comes to laity influencing decisions. Thus the layman and laywoman at
the heart of the particular church are denied their potential for decision-
making and creation of religious content. Nothing remains to them but to be
creators in the marginal sphere of popular Catholicism.[13]

"The only solution," admit Medina and Ribeiro, "lies in an understanding
of the layperson as one of the terms of participating structure—one of the
terms of the power to make decisions bearing on the specific objectives of that
person's church." The researchers continue:

> But to this purpose it is indispensable that the layperson concretely exist as a
> vehicle of religious values in his or her life. The attainment of this will
> involve the alteration of structuration along the prevailing axis: it will mean
> a configuration of the church as a determinate population-totality whose
> constitutive elements, each and all, will have functions differentiated in
> accordance with their position of identical value in the structure. The
> acceptance of such a solution will mean the acceptance as well of alterations
> on the level of the clerical world [bishops, priests] as its frame and function

are redefined. And throughout the whole process, the process of the socialization of the laity will play the key role. Alteration in the mechanism of
religious socialization would be one of the basic requirements for the
functioning of a church with a new identity. A like solution would not alter
the selective nature of the church. The latter would remain differentiated,
but would contain the layperson as a term in an active dimension, as a
vehicle of religious values, and as capable of inspiring the building of the city
of earth.[14]

Thus it is not a matter of despoiling the bishop and priest of their function in
a sham liberation process. It is only that their functions will take on new tasks,
with a new arrangement of relationships among bishop, priest, and layperson.
The theology of Vatican II, initiated in *Lumen Gentium* and in *Apostolicam
Actuositatem* (on the lay apostolate), transcends the linear conception and
supplants it with a triangular one, in which each of *three* terms, this time,
acquires weight of its own and becomes the vehicle and vessel of ecclesial
substance, as Medina and Ribeiro desiderate:

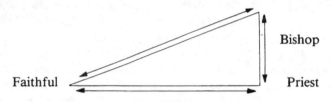

Figure 4. A New Church Structure.

Here all three terms establish a network of relationships with one another,
involving one another in a circularity. As the decree *Ad Gentes* says, "the
Church has not been truly established . . . unless there exists a laity worthy of
the name."[15] All three terms are responsible for the entire reality of church.
Collegiality is no longer the monopoly of episcopate and clergy. Now it belongs
to the whole People of God.

This is the way the basic communities function. Their triangular model has
created a new style of priest and bishop. These are now in the midst of the
people as principles of animation and inspiration, of unity and universality. At
the same time, these communities have caused the laity to emerge as a genuine
vehicle of ecclesiological values, whether as coordinators or moderators of the
community or in the discharge of other community services. In their own
ambit, the laity take up the cause of Christ and share in the decision-making of
their local church. The basic church communities are helping the whole church
in the process of declericalization, by restoring to the People of God, the
faithful, the rights of which they have been deprived in the linear structure. On
the level of theory, theology itself has already gone beyond the old pyramid.
But it is not enough to know. A new praxis must be implemented. This is what
the basic communities are saying. They are helping the whole church to

"reinvent itself," right in its foundations. Experiment is gradually confirming theory, and inspiring in the church-as-institution a confidence in the viability of a new way of being church in the world today.

The basic church communities prefigure a new social structuring of the church. Of course, this new structure will include more than just basic communities. These communities constitute a leaven of renewal in the substance of the whole church—not a global alternative for the totality of the church. José Comblin thinks that we shall have, in the cities, three levels of involvement—of belonging to church—and consequently three types of community. *First*, the basic communities will surely become institutionalized, will expand, will "universalize." Comblin says: "Just as in the Middle Ages the parochial framework structure came in gradually—from the twelfth to the fourteenth centuries—and replaced the old regime of ancient Christianity, so also will the formation of the basic communities be gradual."[16]

Second, we are headed for specialized action groups, springing from the religious institutes and the lay apostolate: teams of priests, study teams, religious centers for spirituality, conversion movements, mission groups, the utilization of television and radio, and the like.

All these kinds of communities already exist. They may be still in embryonic form, but we can already see in them the shape of the church to come. Today's basic communities hold a prophecy, a promise that is slowly becoming historical reality. We shall have a new church, a church born of the faith that nourishes God's People.

4

An Oppressed People Organizing
for Liberation

Dietrich Bonhoeffer, the Protestant theologian, under sentence of death for plotting against Hitler's life, wrote the following prophetic words from prison in 1944:

> It is not for us to prophesy the day (though the day will come) when men will once more be called so to utter the word of God that the world will be changed and renewed by it. It will be a new language, perhaps quite non-religious, but liberating and redeeming—as was Jesus' language; it will shock people and yet overcome them by its power; it will be the language of a new righteousness and truth, proclaiming God's peace with men and the coming of his kingdom. "They shall fear and tremble because of all the good and all the prosperity I provide for it" (Jer. 33:9).[1]

These words seem fulfilled to the letter in the Christianity being lived in thousands of basic church communities across all the working-class neighborhoods of the land. Here the word of God comes to manifestation as a factor for transformation, and for the liberation of the oppressed, striking terror in the hearts of the lovers of the prevailing system and their ideologues.

First Steps

All this is seen in miniature in the Fourth Inter-Church Meeting of the Basic Communities of Brazil, held in Itaici, São Paulo, from April 20 to 24, 1981. In a certain sense, this meeting was the culmination of a journey that had begun in 1975 in Vitória, and spread across the nation. In July of that year, some half-dozen bishops, a few *assessores* (community consultants—*periti*, if you will), a good score of pastoral ministers, and a few members of the basic church communities came together to exchange experiences and reflections on the still emerging, but already vigorous, phenomenon of the *Igreja na base*: the

34

grassroots church, the church of foundations. By far the majority of those participating were from the top of the pyramid, although the sixteen reports they had come to hear were delivered by members of the basic communities themselves, as were the simple stories of actual experiences also related in the joint sessions. It was not hard to see that a true *eclesiogênese*, an "ecclesiogenesis," was under way—the birth, the genesis, of a new church. The word *eclesiogênese*, coined precisely on this occasion, would become a new term in theological parlance. The phenomenon recalls the motto or device of the meeting: *Igreja que Nasce do Povo pelo Espirito de Deus* (Church born of the People through the Spirit of God), which circulated all over the world, provoking certain misunderstandings and even an explicit allusion on the part of the Holy Father in his discourse at the opening of the Puebla conference in 1979.

In July 1976 the Second Inter-Church Meeting was held, once more in Vitória. This time the motto was *Igreja, Povo que Caminha* (The Church, a People on a Journey). The registration profile had changed: half of the 100 participants were from the grassroots communities, and only half consisted of bishops, pastoral ministers, and assessors. Some 100 reports, developed by the grassroots communities themselves, had been sent to the assessors—theologians, educators, sociologists, and so on—for their written comments, which were then returned to the communities for discussion and reflection. This meeting sought to balance the participation of foundation and pinnacle—the floor and the steeple, as we might say—no easy task, considering the diversity of spontaneous levels of discourse.

In July 1978, in João Pessoa, the Third Inter-Church Meeting was held. This time there were some 200 persons in attendance, and two-thirds were "from the pews." The motto was *Igreja, Povo que se Liberta* (The Church, a People Going Free). This time the grassroots church came to full expression. Representatives of the communities organized everything, coordinating the groups, making the presentations, and joining together to work out the final document. The unheard-of was happening: after 480 years of silence, a religious, oppressed people had the floor, and the monopoly of the corpus of church experts on speech was over. Catechist, priest, and bishop were no longer the only ones with the gift of speech. Assessors, pastoral ministers, and bishops could hear from the lips of the people themselves all about their economic, political, and cultural despoiling, could hear their cries for justice and participation. On two points opinion was unanimous: (1) the main root of this oppression is the elitist, exclusive, capitalist system; and (2) people resist and are liberated to the extent that they unite and create a network of popular movements. The analysis of the 200 grassroots reports by the *periti* present has yielded the best writing in ecclesiology in recent years, and the material has been translated into a number of languages.

The Fourth Inter-Church Meeting, held in Itaici in 1981, was a veritable celebration of the power of participation and organization lodging in the grassroots. Bishops (including a cardinal, Lorscheider), assessors, and community representatives totaled some 300 persons from 71 dioceses and 19 regions of the country. As in João Pessoa, here too those "from the pews" coordinated and conducted the meeting right to the end.

"Survivors of the Great Period of Trial"

Anyone seeing these hundreds of people, humble and lowly, bearing the marks of poverty, with simple wooden sandals on their feet, their faces furrowed with the struggle to live, cheerful and animated, chatting with one another as if they had been old friends, would have recalled that celebrated multitude in the book of Revelation: "Who are these people . . . ? And where have they come from? . . . These are the ones who have survived the great period of trial . . . "(Rev. 7:13–14).

From remote corners of the land they came, from the poor suburbs of the cities, these survivors of hard battles for existence, these beloved of God because of being poor, these whom "the Lamb on the throne will shepherd . . . lead them to springs of life-giving water, and God will wipe every tear from their eyes" (Rev. 7:17). Indeed, the four days of the meeting were quite a shock for anyone not of the grassroots. The competence and maturity with which the small-group and general sessions were conducted was impressive, as was the deftness with which problems were presented as playlets, or the enthusiasm of the prayerful songs composed by musicians and poets of the people in the communities themselves. Special mention should be made of the celebrations with which each day's work began and ended. The whole mystique, the whole religiousness of a people appeared here. Their awareness of their identity as church was obvious. The struggles of which we heard in the small groups were celebrated and ritualized, either in processions about the gardens of the huge monastery, or at the Offertory, when the problems that had come up in the discussions were made the subject of spontaneous petition in the Prayer of the Faithful.

No one wished to be anyone's teacher. All sought to be disciples of all. Bishops and assessors spoke only when called upon to do so, or when they lined up with everyone else to wait their turn. Surely not a few will long have engraved in their memories the moving spectacle of the dramatic presentations of the struggles of the people, playlets improvised on the spot—for this was no theater, this was real life, the story of Xoco Indians, armed with slingshots, facing police with rifles and machine-guns, defending their lands, or recovering the statue of Saint Peter, which had been stolen from them. After each story, as in Homeric times, a song was sung, composed as a victory celebration. All present sang the Xoco refrain:

> Saint Peter, you're not alone,
> There are Xocos all around!

Nor was it less worthy of astonishment and admiration to see the masters and fathers of the faith—the bishops—at the feet of the lowly, hearing their testimony, following their reflections, and learning truly evangelical lessons. The cardinal archbishop of São Paulo, Paulo Evaristo, put it very well: "The cardinal admires and supports you, and seeks to learn from you!"

Unlike what many might have thought, there was nothing about the participants to indicate any threat of breach with the oneness of the church. On the contrary, with great maturity and critical distance, the participants discussed tensions existing among various pastoral approaches, the resistance of some to accepting the approach of a people who become People of God by way of the basic communities, or the authoritarian attitudes of certain bishops who still cling to a triumphalist conceptualization of church. Such obstacles were viewed as inevitable on any journey, hence not to be taken too dramatically. The plenary assembly voted to write the pope a letter, thanking him for the greeting he had addressed to the communities in Manaus, and containing a declaration of loyalty to the great apostolic tradition whose guarantor the pope was.

Obstacles to Understanding Basic Church Communities

Before undertaking a detailed analysis of some of the points raised in the Itaici meeting, it will be in order to attempt to do away with certain preconceptions sometimes entertained concerning the basic communities, preconceptions that present an obstacle to a more objective evaluation of their relevance. Gaston Bachelard, the great modern French epistemologist, has shown us that science has in large part been built upon the effort to destroy errors, and that an approximative objective knowledge of reality is achieved by overcoming certain basic epistemological obstacles. This applies to an understanding of the phenomenon of the basic church communities, too. These have been the object of open polemics and attacks on the part of certain sectors of the world press. It would behoove us all to arm ourselves with clarity and objectivity. It would be sad indeed to have to see this reality of a suffering people misunderstood once more, and perhaps even deprived of the new hope that is theirs. The oppressed must not be cheated of their hope, especially when it is such a fragile hope, born from the actual struggles of resistance and liberation of the people themselves.

1. The first obstacle has to do with an understanding of the nature of the basic church communities. We are not dealing with a movement in the church like the Cursillo Movement, the Christian Catechumenate, or the Christian Family Movement. With the basic communities we are faced with something more fundamental. These are church itself, among the people, in the church's foundations. The basic communities are a response to the question: How may the community experience of the apostolic faith be embodied and structured in the conditions of a people who, in Brazil as throughout Latin America, are both religious and oppressed? The church communities, as Pope John Paul II emphasized in his message to the Manaus communities, are genuinely church assimilating the characteristics of the people, church in which the people can

express their faith in a key that belongs to their own culture, to their own values, to their yearning for a liberation that will bring participation and communion in justice. These communities do not, therefore, constitute a reality that may simply be thrust aside or submitted to the simple decision of a bishop whether or not they are to be accepted. In proportion as the greater church opens out to the popular echelons, the popular echelons confer their own earmark on the greater church. Thus the greater church may not refuse to become a church of the people if it seeks actually to evangelize this people, these poor, who constitute the vast majority of persons in Latin America. When it does so refuse, the Christian people are reduced to a throng of clientele, customers, without any further share in the dynamic makeup of the church itself.

2. The second obstacle concerns the liberative import of Christian faith. We are the heirs of a codification of faith that has concentrated particularly on the call of faith to a person in his or her individuality, or to the family as privileged medium of transmission of the Christian faith and ethos. This form of Christianity has not thoroughly explored the liberative dimensions of faith—the so-called "perilous, subversive memory of Jesus Christ" who was crucified by the powers of this world and raised up by God to demonstrate the divine and human triumph of a life sacrificed for the cause of the total liberation of human beings, especially of the impoverished. The Puebla conference harshly criticized this reduction of Christianity to the intimate sphere of private life. Jesus preached and died in public, out in the world, and he is Lord not only of the little corners of our hearts, but of society and the cosmos as well. Christian faith develops and proclaims a message concerned with the absolute and ultimate aspect of human life in God. This is obvious. But this absolute and ultimate element is linked to, and depends on, the way we lead our lives in its penultimate and antepenultimate moments and instances. It depends on how we conduct our lives in history. The Christian message, then, proclaims not only the world's happy dénouement, but the urgent call to involvement in the world on its way to this dénouement. It preaches not only resurrection, but the just quality of a temporal life of human beings. From this flows a determined faith commitment to social processes that aim at the building of more symmetrical, more humane social relationships. One need not be a Christian to be a good politician. The Scholastics of the Middle Ages knew this and taught it. But to be a good Christian, it is necessary to be concerned with social justice, and social justice is a political reality. In order to achieve this social justice, so wanting in today's discriminatory society, one must live the faith as a factor of transformation of social relationships. Christians in the Brazilian reality who oppose qualitative changes in society are not just conservative citizens. They are Christians disloyal to the gospel, since they are being deaf to the cry of the oppressed that rises up on all sides. A Christianity that has made people aware of this demand for change is no longer available for use as a totem legitimating the social and religious status quo. It has emerged as a factor for protest and for the development of liberative ideas. This is what is occurring in the basic

church communities, deeply, consistently. Here practical alternatives spring from a living evangelical experience of faith—in response to a prophetic denunciation of the abuses of the system in all its antipopular structure—with courage, but without great social resonance. As one participant in the Itaici meeting put it, "Our communities sprang up because we were hungry for God's word. Then we saw that liberation was next." This social task, flowing from a faith that has taken flesh in conflictual reality, does no harm to the dimension of prayer and celebration. On the contrary, our experience helps us to pray in a deeper way. As a participant from Paraiba said: "When the big farm gobbled us up, and the goons were threatening us because we resisted, we kept always praying, and looking for light in the word of the Bible, which is the word of God." It is precisely the liberation theologians who write most about spirituality, mysticism, and prayer, as a demand for social commitment on the part of anyone wishing to preserve the Christian identity.

A third obstacle to an understanding of the communities flows from an illuministic preconception that still persists in some circles of the church, and more broadly among intellectuals directly bound to the interests of the economico-political system under which we live and suffer. As the best contemporary Brazilian historian, José Honório Rodriques, has bluntly put it:

> The dominant minority—conservative or liberal—has always been alienated, antiprogressive, antinational, and uncontemporary . . . . The leadership has never become reconciled with the people. It has never seen the people as creatures of God, has never recognized them for what they are, since the leadership would like them to be what they are not. It has never seen their virtues, or admired their services to the country. It calls them all "Jeca-Tatus," country yokels, denies them their rights, ruins their lives, and then, when it sees them "on their way up" in spite of everything, gradually withdraws its patronage and conspires to remand them once more to the periphery—to where it has always really felt they belonged in the first place.[2]

Let us note that many criticisms of the basic communities are extensions of this tradition of certain intellectuals who are organically linked to dominant power, with their gratuitous illuministic premise that they alone are the vessels of wisdom, light, and solutions. The people, they say, need supervision, control, orientation—presupposing, of course, that the people know nothing, that they are still minors and need guardians, that the laity lack the necessary orientation, and that priests will have to be present in these community cells on a daily basis in order to preserve orthodoxy. Here we may see the corruption of the elite, the intelligentsia, for whom democracy and wisdom are mutually exclusive. Our wise mentors have even reached such a pitch of absurdity as to deny the people the right to meet and to work out their own reflections—thus these mentors place themselves at odds with the most basic democratic ideal, which ought to be valid for all cases, even the economic. The allegation that the common people fall prey to deviations is half true. Deviations are always possible, in any historical process, on the part of the people as well as on the part of their guides. Laity and bishops alike may deviate. A mutual apprenticeship, in mutual openness, is the best means whereby to avoid deviations on either side. Evangelization is a two-way street. The bishop evangelizes the people, and the people evangelize the bishop. Otherwise, who evangelizes the bishop? Who sees to his salvation? After all, salvation is not bestowed on one just because one is a bishop. Salvation comes with being a good Christian, one who is just, who respects the rights of human beings (especially the poor), who is faithful to the criteria of evangelical practice. This applies as well to the Christian called to discharge the service of bishop, as principle of unity, doctrinal unity included, in the community.

Unless these and other obstacles to an understanding of the basic church communities are overcome, it will be difficult indeed to grasp the paramount significance of these communities for the church and society.

The Church: An Oppressed People Organizing for Liberation

Now that we have sought to clarify three main obstacles to an understanding of the basic communities, we may address the more relevant points of the Fourth Inter-Church Meeting, held in Itaici. The central theme was *Igreja, Povo Oprimido que se Organiza para a Libertação* (The Church, an Oppressed People Organizing for Liberation). This theme was divided into subthemes, one for each of the four days of the meeting: Day 1, participation in the church; Day 2, solidarity in the local community; Day 3, service in the realm of politics; Day 4, justice in the working world. From this writer's point of view as a theological assessor, the results of the meeting could be summed up under the following five heads.

Faith and Celebrations of Faith Are Essential

The main thing to emerge from all four Inter-Church meetings, not just from the one in Itaici, was the dimension and celebration of faith. These are of the essence. They are not adventitious or "accidental." They are part of what defines the specific character of the communities. The communities are *churches*, and this is the title their members claim for them. What brings them together is hunger for the word of God. What we have here is a faith that is whole and complete, without euphemisms or dissimulation. Persons coming from intellectual, secularized, a-religious, skeptical, or gnostic milieus, to whom "the religious" says little or nothing, are profoundly astonished to find communities in which faith is altogether stranger to saccharine pietism, communities where faith makes bold to define the sense of all existence and the orientation of all practice. People perceive this dimension of faith not only when they talk about the Bible, with which everyone is more or less familiar, but even more when they talk about life-problems: land, salaries, unions.

Biblical references are everywhere. They are used for finding today's pharaohs and today's prophets. They are used for discerning those who are working to build up the kingdom, a process which always passes by way of the mediation of justice and love, of the practice of solidarity and a communion of persons. One perceives that faith is not just a frill on life's lapel, but the horizon against which all things are globalized—without denying secular or political reality their autonomous density. But any parallelism or juxtaposition of the religious and the secular, of cult and ethic, so widespread in the "intimist" Christianity of bourgeois circles, is shunned. Here the God-dimension does justice to God as the all-embracing Reality, respecting God's special place in all things, and making it possible to see even the political and the economic as mediations of God's grace or of dis-grace, in proportion as the *humanum* is accorded or denied the justice and dignity that are its due. Because this profound unity—not identification, but unity—between faith and life prevails, celebrations win an altogether special relevance. They become something more than the execution of a venerable rite. Life is celebrated, the life of a faith lived in the struggles of the everyday, and the ones celebrating are the people, these people so filled with drama and tragedy. As the bishops testified in a joint letter:

> The most profound experiences of the day in Itaici were without a doubt the celebrations in the morning, and especially the Eucharist in the evening. They were encounters of a deep, joyful faith, where, in the Paschal Mystery, everything was celebrated that had happened during the day. The participation of the congregation was extremely lively—sometimes all but uncontained. Tirelessly the people praised, gave thanks, and petitioned their God and Father. Indeed, it is from this innermost wellspring of Christian identity that these "little brothers and sisters of Jesus" draw their greatest strength and their highest hopes.

The Social Flows from the Religious

One is often struck by the acute social awareness prevailing in the communities. Itaici was anything but an exception. This "raised consciousness" is not the fruit of some leftist ideological infiltration, but of the reading of the handbook of the faith, the Bible, and of an attempt to understand it in the context in which it was written. The Bible was written in communities of poor people, nearly always under the domination of foreign powers and yearning for integral liberation. At Itaici one would hear, "God is political, but he's fair—look at Exodus 3:7: 'I have witnessed the affliction of my people in Egypt, and have heard their cry of complaint against their slave drivers. . . . Therefore I have come down to rescue them . . . ' " (Exod. 3:7–8). Or "Jesus was a hundred per cent political. Look at John 10:10: 'The thief comes only to steal and slaughter and destroy, I came that they might have life and have it to the full.' And what's politics but generating life, in justice and love?" Faith generates commitment to the transformation of society as a way of preparing material for the kingdom here and now—for this kingdom is already beginning, here on earth. This reading of the faith is something these people have acquired and embodied in their lives and experiences.

The Capitalist System Must Be Attacked in Its Roots

When it comes to identifying the causes of the miseries they suffer, the members of the basic communities see the main one—not the only one, but the main one—as the capitalist system. But worse than the system itself is its individualistic spirit of accumulation, its social irresponsibility, and its insensitivity toward human beings, who are treated as "manpower" to be sold at auction. The communities denounce this as unjust, as contrary to God's design in history. From the poor who had come together in Itaici, we heard tales of the most unbelievable violence, perpetrated by a capitalism as savage as that of the English in Manchester, India, or China. This was not the well-behaved neo-capitalism of Senator Jarbas Passarinho, leader of the current military-style government. This was the cruel, uncontrolled appropriation of the interior of our country by rampant capitalist relations of production. The people have harsh words for this. There is no cure for this system. It must be overcome. As for the powers that be—the agents of this system, be they the government authorities themselves—the people are not superstitious. They criticize them directly. No longer is domination internalized here. It is extrojected, along with the dominator, who has so long maintained these people in a state of subjection by means of fetishes. This attitude is now part and parcel of the view of society as developed in our communities. Let there be no illusions on this point: this does not mean Marxism, it just means Gospel—the Gospel read in the context of inequitable oppression.

Interrelationships of the Communities with Popular Movements

Another point became very clear in the small-group sessions as well as in the general ones. The people's strength for resistance and liberation is in proportion to their ability to unify their communities with one another and with the popular movements. It is no wonder, then, that some dozen union leaders, along with well over a score of other officeholders, plus activists from popular parties and leaders of neighborhood associations, were present at the Itaici meeting. Armed violence was never encouraged. Nor was crime. Nor was any other means that the powerful use with such little scruple.

A member from Goiás put it well: "The people go out to meet the police and the goons with the peace of Jesus Christ." He explained what he meant by the peace of Jesus Christ. It meant "putting our farm tools—our mattocks, our tractors, whatever we can find—along with our elderly, our children, and our wives in the path of the armed attackers," and creating human roadblocks. We heard story after story, like stations of a people's Way of the Cross. They showed the effectiveness of union and vigorous resistance. One of the songs most often sung in Itaici came from the communities of Paraíba. It was written by Bishop José Maria Pires:

> I believe there'll be a better world
> When the littlest one who falls
> Believes in that little one—
> When the small can trust that all will be well for each,
> When we feel each other's needs:
> One in Jesus Christ, one with everyone.

Politics, the Mighty Weapon

A great recovery of the noble sense of politics is under way in the communities. So is a quest for the common good of the whole people. This is what is brought into being with the creation of communities—associations of every kind, for whatever may refashion the social fabric and rebuild the people permanently, as agents of their own fate, coresponsible for the building of a livable communality for all. This is what the group meant when it spelled "politics" with a capital P in their final letter: "And Politics is the mighty weapon we have, to build a just society the way God wants it."

On the other hand, it was equally clear that the church community as a religious body could not turn itself into a party cell. Not that this exempted it from rendering a critical judgment on the various parties and their programs, or from unmasking their underlying interests and what type of connection they have with the people. On the contrary, it demands this. Members are free to vote whatever ticket they please. But the level of awareness developed in the communities inclines members to support "parties that really are of the people and defend the interests and rights of the working people." There is no great enthusiasm for big campaigns, however, no infection with the electric excitement of mass movements—things more typical of a populism with the dominant class at the helm. The people have been crushed too often and too cruelly to allow themselves to succumb to such illusions. Projects like these are the product of the imagination of an intelligentsia that is simply out of touch with the real movement of the people. As one of the Itaici participants said so well: "I take my time, because I'm in such a hurry to have liberation." A word that comes up again and again in the communities is *caminhada*: "journey." The people are indeed aware of the burdensome nature of their journey, a journey of resistance and struggle, not of facile enthusiasm.

The New Barbarians

It is easy to see, from what has been said, that the meaning of the basic church communities transcends their religious limits. They are giving birth to the new Christian, the one with the "new language, . . . liberating and redeeming—as was Jesus' language; . . . the language of a new righteousness and truth," which Bonhoeffer, the prophetic theologian, so ardently longed for.[3] But this Christian is a citizen, too, and a critical, participating, democratic citizen—the agent not of a pre-established system, but of a new social hope. And these are the lowliest of our people. These are the "new barbarians," rocking the empire to its foundations with a creativity that portends the advent of a new society. They are the emerging new historical agents, coming to join everyone else on society's "floor" who is organizing and struggling for a different society. We cannot say, of course, what the future society will be. But from the look of the mighty hope sown here, we can say that it will surely be a more participatory one, and much more a community of brothers and sisters than the society that we have inherited from our nations and our forebears. When the people organize, they show what society ought to be: strong and invincible.

5

Quaestio Disputata I:
Did the Historical Jesus Will Only
One Institutional Form for the Church?

Introduction

Throughout our reflections thus far, we have omitted certain problems on which divergent but legitimate opinions prevail among theologians and currents of theological thought. Which particular model we choose for our understanding of faith, or Christianity, or the future of the church is not a matter of indifference for the solutions we actually give to these "disputed questions." But still less will our solutions be indifferent for the decisions we shall be making in the pastoral area.

For example, we have stated that the basic church communities are tantamount to the church reinvented. Here many will ask: Is it possible to reinvent the church? Was not the church founded once and for all by Jesus Christ, and handed down to human beings with all of its basic structures? Are not the episcopate, the priesthood, and the sacraments of divine institution? Can such essential elements in the church be tampered with?

Here is another example, this one from Carlos Mesters, a Dutch missionary and scripture scholar who has spent many years working with Brazilian base communities:

[We have] the concrete problem of the priest crushed by the weight of sacramentalization. The sacraments pertain to a kind of interior warehouse of the life of the community, and this life may not be allowed to be dependent on the clergy as a class. Without this interior life, the community will never be able to do anything, will never arrive at a real autonomy. The clergy have become a class, and, as a class, have monopolized, accumulated in their own hands, the administration of the sacraments. They have become something like the man with the key to the service station, without being the

45

owner of the station, and have created in the people a consciousness of total dependency on "Father" for the means to get to God. The time has come to eliminate the Operator and set up a direct-dial system for the people. This means (1) that the people will be able to rediscover the sacramental (symbolic) meaning and sense of life; (2) that clericalism (not the ministerial priesthood) will be eliminated from the administration of the sacraments (which is not the same thing as handing it over to trained laity); (3) that the people will be able to become the proprietors of their own sacraments—to run the service station themselves.[1]

In these concrete words of Mesters we have the whole problem. But the question arises: Can the church do this? What sort of church did Jesus wish his church to be? Indeed, did Jesus will any particular institutional framework for it at all? The answer conditions the answers to all the problems that we have been raising in this book. Today, with the ministerial crisis in the church and with the effervescence of the basic communities and their particular forms of organization, these problems become very real. By no means are they theoretical.

We have stated that the church is a structured community, and we stand by our statement. But this is where a serious problem of accent arises. In this structured community, which element receives the emphasis—the structure or the community? There are those who place the accent on structure, in which case the church starts from the top down: pope to bishop to priest to brother or nun to laity. This is the official version, and has prevailed in the West for centuries. Then there are those who emphasize community. Here the image of church that is sketched is one of the fellowship of all members; it is a circular, participatory model. Any hierarchical structure occurring within the community is for the good of the community. Before hierarchies and differences, Jesus sought to introduce fellowship, participation, community.

We now propose to approach—in the form of *quaestiones disputatae*, as there are differing legitimate opinions on each—a number of current issues: first, the matter of the relationship of the historical Jesus with the institutional church; second, whether or not a layperson can celebrate the Lord's Supper; and finally, the question of women's priesthood.

In this chapter we shall explore the first question, which is also the chapter title: Did the historical Jesus will only one institutional form for the church?

In faith we say that Jesus Christ founded the church. This is a correct statement, and it expresses the 2,000-year-old faith of the church. However—and here is the problem—this statement is neither unambiguous nor simple. There are some steps missing, and these have to be clarified in order for the statement to have dogmatic meaning as a basic assertion.

"Christ founded the church. The church was founded in Christ and by Christ." Let us take a closer look at a rather general tendency in Catholic theology today when it comes to the subject of the historical Jesus and the church-as-institution. As we have said, this is a *quaestio disputata*. Ours is not the only legitimate opinion, nor even the only respectable one. But the solution we shall propose will help us to contextualize and theologically base the ecclesiogenesis and reinvention of the church as we defend it. We are witnessing a new birth of the church. The church may now take a different form. After all, there is room for this in ecclesiology. It is the intention of Jesus Christ that there be. This statement is based on representative views in Catholic theology and exegesis.

The problem of the relationship between the historical Jesus and the church can be formulated as a radical, basic question: Did the historical, pre-Easter Jesus will a church? This question is provocative; it is also ambiguous—as ambiguous as the word "church" itself. If by "church" we mean grace, liberation, the irruption of the Spirit, the new creation, the heavenly Jerusalem, and the kingdom of God, then Christ willed the church. Indeed there is nothing else in this world he did will, in his life, message, death, and resurrection.

But if by "church" we understand the visible institution, its sacramental organization, its hierarchical ministerial institution, its sociological structures as the service of the grace of the kingdom, its theological self-understanding, then this question takes on a very different look. It becomes a historical question rather than a systematic one—although of course the historical response will have tremendous influence on the systematic understanding of what the church is and should be.

Hermeneutical Presuppositions for an Answer

The sources for our study of this question will be the Gospels. But these sources cannot be dealt with simply as "history books." They constitute a category apart: that of witness to and propagation of the faith. In order to make use of the Gospels as sources for historical data, therefore, we must take into account the following six hermeneutical presuppositions of Catholic exegesis as generally practiced and taught today.

1. The Gospels were written after Jesus' death and resurrection. These two events profoundly modified the understanding that the apostles had of Jesus.

2. A great proportion of the Gospel material was developed after the destruction of Jerusalem, an event that brought with it a new understanding of Jesus' message. At first that message was carried by Jews to Jews. Now, however, Jerusalem, and everything that Jerusalem meant theologically as the center of the world and the place of the manifestation of God, was without a future.

3. A great proportion of the Gospel material was redacted only after the development of a church organization, and after the beginning of mission to and conversion of Gentiles. All of this is reflected in the text and theology of the respective evangelists.

4. The Gospel texts reflect a different atmosphere regarding future expecta-

tions from the one in which Jesus lived. Jesus lived in an atmosphere of the eschatological imminence of the irruption of the kingdom. The Gospels, by contrast, are written under the sign of the postponement of the Parousia, or second coming of Christ—which now would not occur until some unknown time in the distant future. The very fact that Gospels were developed at all testifies to a conviction that the end was not imminent. The community was organizing to face the concrete problems and history into which the church would now enter.

5. The actual Gospel texts are testimonials of faith. That is, they not only report a past, but seek to explain a present lived in the light of what has appeared in the past: the Christ's preaching, death, and resurrection. They represent the encounter of church organization and Jesus' message. Intertwined with all the blocks of historical content, then, these texts include theology: reflection and interpretation in the light of what had been and experienced in the days when Jesus still walked among his disciples. The Gospels make no distinction between the Jesus of history and the Christ of faith, between what is of Jesus and what is of the faith community. Both elements are indifferently attributed to Christ. Obviously this makes the work of the historian much more difficult. Analysis will have to distinguish between what probably originates with the historical Jesus and what is to be attributed to the theological or redactional labors of the evangelist or community. Thus it can happen that texts which, on their face, and traditionally, seem to report the *ipsissima verba Jesu*, Jesus' historical words, must, in virtue of these critical presuppositions, be considered as theological elaborations of the primitive community.

6. The evangelists did what Paul did. They interpreted Jesus' message. And we are still doing this, in theology, catechetics, and, especially, homiletics. Nor is there anything else we could do, for understanding is always a vital process of interpretation. Our homilies are not a recital of the past. They are a proclamation of the present. They are the confrontation of our ongoing history with the message we have heard. When we preach, we are convinced that, in spite of all interpretation, we are not teaching our own doctrine and message, but merely articulating, in a different time and language, the original faith message of the Gospels. We find the same process in the New Testament. It could not have been any other way.

With all this presupposed, then, we can now reflect upon the relationship between the historical Jesus and the church.

Image of the Church in the "Theology of Tranquillity"

There is a "theology of tranquillity" that represents the church as being in perfect continuity with the work of Jesus. It runs somewhat as follows: Jesus came to save human beings by his death and resurrection. He founded the church, during his earthly life, to continue his work until the consummation of the ages. To this purpose he endowed it with ministries and sacraments and dogmatic and moral teaching in order to actualize his salvation and render it present in the world. The church is united to its Founder in such wise that it can be called the body of Christ ontologically.

We do not question the dogmatic validity of this representation of the church. But we do wonder whether it correctly reflects the Gospels. We must keep an open mind, so as to be able to understand, from a point of departure in Jesus' message, whether what the church is or ought to be today is actually what is traditionally presented. We must remember that the Gospels have a different idea of church from the one commonly held by the faithful. One need only reflect, for example, that, of the four evangelists, only Saint Matthew speaks of a "church" (Mt. 16:18, 18:17). Saint Luke never uses the word *ekklēsia* in his Gospel; by contrast, in the Acts of the Apostles he uses it a score of times. Is he not telling us that the church is not something from the time of the historical Jesus, but from the time after Pentecost? Hans Conzelmann has shown us clearly the neat distinction introduced by Luke between the time of Jesus and the time of the church. They are two different salvific historical situations.[2] The church, then, is not a creation of the time of Jesus, but a creation of the time of the Spirit.

For the evangelists, there is a breach, a "rupture," between Jesus and the church. Between these two events comes the "failure" of Jesus crucified, together with the faithlessness of the apostles and the dissolution of the community of Jesus' followers. Only after the resurrection did Jesus' followers come together again.

Jesus' Ultimate Intent: Not the Church, but the Kingdom of God

These few observations raise a question. Does the foundation of the church belong to the time of the historical Jesus, or is it a post-Paschal phenomenon?

In order to respond to this momentous query, it will not be enough to settle the much debated problem whether Matthew 16:18–19 (". . . You are 'Rock,' and upon this rock I will build my church. . . . I will entrust to you the keys of the kingdom of heaven.") is authentically from Jesus or not. Far more radical questions have to be considered. For example:

1. If Jesus considered himself sent only to Israel (cf. Mt. 10:5–6; 15:24), and to the totality of Israel, how could he have envisaged the foundation of a community of faithful formed of his disciples and future followers which would be one among so many in Israel—the "sect of the Nazarenes" (Acts 24:5,14)?

2. If Jesus' perspective was one of an imminent eschatology, then how could he have thought of a pilgrim church perduring down through the course of the ages, institutionally organized and historically so rigidly defined?

3. If Jesus' preaching concentrated on the idea of the kingdom of God, and if the kingdom of God had a universal, cosmic connotation, then how do we get a church as a reduced, ambiguous realization of the kingdom of God?

Alfred Loisy (1857–1940), the modernist, stated the problem well when he wrote, somewhat disconcertedly: "Christ preached the Kingdom of God, and the Church appeared instead."[3] Catholic exegesis has taken this problem seriously for a long time. We need only recall the two classic works of the renowned Catholic exegete Rudolf Schnackenburg: *God's Rule and Kingdom* and *The Church in the New Testament*.[4] Schnackenburg says that, following the New Testament, we must clearly distinguish between the *basileia tou Theou*—the kingdom of God—and the *ekklēsia tou Theou*: "It is not the Church but the kingdom of God which is the ultimate goal of the divine economy of salvation and redemption in its perfect form for the whole world."[5]

If the kingdom of God and the church are not perfectly identical, however, what relationship does obtain between them? How do we get from Christ's preaching on the kingdom to the establishment of the church? Is the latter an immediate consequence of the former, or does it merely constitute a flimsy substitute for the kingdom of God, which cannot be seen? Is the church the fruit of a "disappointment" or of a fulfillment?

Catholic exegetical studies on the church in the New Testament are unanimous on two points.[6] First, one may speak of the church only from the resurrection onward. Second, this church is understood as the eschatological salvation-community. In the words of Schnackenburg:

> We can speak of church in the proper sense, as the community of Christ, only after the elevation of Christ and the coming of the Holy Spirit. The community of the disciples around the historical Jesus is not yet church, the community of the redeemed in the future kingdom is no longer church.[7]

Anton Vögtle expresses it still more straightforwardly:

> The totality of primitive Christianity speaks of church only from the moment of Christ's resurrection. The church, for the New Testament witnesses, is conditioned in its existence by the death and resurrection of Jesus. It is clearly a post-Easter quantity.[8]

In function of these findings in the area of exegesis, Hans Küng, in his book on ecclesiology, feels on solid ground in formulating this proposition: "*In the pre-Easter period*, during his lifetime, *Jesus did not found a Church. . . .* by his preaching and ministry, [he] *laid the foundations* for the emergence of a post-resurrection Church."[9] Jesus' death and faith in his resurrection are the foundation of the church. Without faith in the resurrection, it would be incomprehensible that the community would reassemble and preach the crucified One as the Messiah. Jesus' cause and person were not over with his death. Both reappeared after the resurrection, as begetters and constituents of the church community.

There is a discontinuity, then, between the preaching of the kingdom and the church. This discontinuity is constituted by Jesus' death on the cross. There is also a continuity between Jesus and the church. This continuity is constituted by the resurrection, through which Christ continues his presence. The articulation of the continuity and the discontinuity between Jesus and the church is the theological task of any ecclesiology claiming to be based on the New Testament.

Did Jesus Preach the Kingdom of God or the Church?

Jesus did not go forth to preach the church, but to preach the kingdom of God. "This is the time of fulfillment. The reign of God is at hand! Reform your lives and believe in the gospel!" (Mk. 1:15).

Eschatological and Universal Content of the Kingdom of God

"Kingdom of God" and "reign of God" on the lips of Jesus are an eschatological concept. "It means," wrote Bultmann, "the regime of God which will destroy the present course of the world, wipe out all the contra-divine, Satanic power under which the present world groans—and thereby, terminating all pain and sorrow, bring in salvation for the People of God which awaits the fulfilment of the prophets' promises."[10]

"Kingdom of God" does not mean a national theocracy, nor does it mean a territory. Nor, on the other hand, does it denote something purely spiritual. It means a new world order, where God is all in all (cf. 1 Cor. 15:28). The kingdom of God is not a reward for the devout and a chastisement for sinners. It is practically the contrary: it is Good News for sinners, and for all willing to be converted. The preaching of the kingdom is addressed to all Israel, not just a part. Conversion is required of all, sinful and devout, which implies that all Israel needs converting and that no one as yet belongs to the kingdom. Here we see the concrete universalism of Jesus' preaching.[11] If all Israel needs a change in its life, we reflect, how much more the Gentiles!

Jesus' universalism is intensive, not extensive, however. His preaching is actually addressed only to the Jews, and not to a church of Jews and Gentiles. The latter was not within the scope of his intent. He had no intention of founding a new faith community alongside the others of his time, each of which already claimed for itself the title of "true Israel." *Jesus sought to convert all Israel.* In this sense, he did not will a church as a group different from one of believing Jews. Furthermore, the notion of the kingdom of God embraces all reality, including infrahuman reality, inasmuch as this reality too is to be purified of its evil and inserted into God's absolute lordship.

Eschatological Sign: Constitution of the Twelve

Could one perhaps think that the constitution of the Twelve (Mk. 3:14) meant a small ecclesial community, the future community in germ and seed?[12] Here we must be on our guard. We must not retroject that post-Easter development, the church, into the time of the historical Jesus. It is true that the Lord "named twelve"—or "made twelve," *epoiēsen dōdeka*, as the Greek original would have it (Mk. 3:14)—and sent them to preach the kingdom (Mt. 10:5–6). It was not communitarian functions that were created for them, however, but a symbolic one. The Twelve symbolize the eschatological reconstitution of the twelve tribes of Israel, of which only two-and-one-half were left in the time of Christ: "You who have followed me shall likewise take your places on twelve thrones to judge the twelve tribes of Israel" (Mt. 19:28; cf. Lk. 22:30). *The importance of the Twelve resides in being twelve, not in being apostles.* Saint Mark never speaks of the twelve "apostles," but only of the "twelve" (Mk. 3:14,16; 4:10; 6:7–35; 9:35; 10:32; 11:11; 14:10–17). Only after the resurrection was there mission and then the little group was transformed into apostles— persons sent. It was in his reflection upon the post resurrection mission that Matthew could compose Jesus' long discourse on mission (Mt. 9:35–10:40). The actual words are without doubt those of the evangelist.[13]

The Twelve thus stand in a relationship with all Israel—and not with a group apart, within Israel, constituting a community we should call a church in miniature. They share in Christ's task of preaching the kingdom, but their function is that of "multipliers," to help this message reach more parts of Israel. The institution of the Twelve is altogether in keeping with Jesus' eschatological horizon, the same horizon we find in the community of Qumran, where there was also a college of twelve, alongside another one of three—the same symbolic structure.[14] The Twelve constitute a sign of the fact that the kingdom is being realized for all Israel, and it is here that their theological significance resides. "Apostle," by contrast, is a post-Paschal mission concept.

Peter the Rock, Foundation of the Faith of the Easter Church

Some people may argue that Jesus founded the church when he made his promise to Peter: "I for my part declare to you, you are 'Rock,' and on this rock I will build my church, and the jaws of death shall not prevail against it" (Mt. 16:18).

Let us first observe that the older version, in Mark, has Peter's confession but not Christ's promise (Mk. 8:27–30; cf. Lk. 9:18–21). The promise is *Sondergut* (special material proper to one evangelist only, in this case Matthew). For the exegesis of this difficult passage we follow three Catholic exegetes in particular: R. Pesch, J. Blank, and P. V. Dias.[15] In the judgment of both Dias and Pesch, the honorific name *Kephas—Petros*, Peter, Rock—did not originate with Jesus. Except in Luke 22:34, Jesus always calls the apostle "Simon" in the Gospels. Simon owes his name Kephas to the fact of having been the first witness of the resurrection (cf. 1 Cor. 15:5; Lk. 24:34). Dias writes, "With Peter, faith in the Resurrection began, and therewith the history of Christ's church."[16] He is the rock upon which the church will stand through all the centuries, for it will be built upon faith in the resurrection as first testified to by Peter. Peter is thus the first Christian. He strengthens his sisters and brothers in the faith (Lk. 22:32). He also guides and directs them (Jn.

21:15-17). The explanation of Peter as the rock-foundation of the church is an etiological one. Peter has received this name in the community because of his profession of faith in Jesus' resurrection. Upon this profession a church is built, and the powers of the ages will never be able to prevail against it.[17]

It is likewise noteworthy that the promise made to Peter is made in Caesarea Philippi—mission territory. Here we may perhaps understand an endorsement of the mission, headed by Peter, which left Jerusalem for Antioch. It is upon Peter's missionary decision, Matthew implies, that the church will be built: a church of Jews and Gentiles alike. Indeed, the prophecy that the church would be built on Peter—upon his missionary decision and faith profession—has been realized in history.

The power of the keys entrusted to Peter (Mt. 16:19) in Matthew's commu- . nity signifies doctrinal authority.[18] Peter is the representative and guarantor of Jesus' teaching, and of its interpretation as collated in Saint Matthew's Gospel. Thus as Paul is the guarantor of the orthodox teaching for the communities of pastoral letters, so Peter is guarantor for that teaching in Matthew's community. It is also to be noted that the same power of binding and loosing as is conferred on Peter is also ascribed to the whole community (Mt. 18:18). For Matthew, Peter is representative and guarantor—rather than head—of the community.

Matthew 16:18-19 is a post-Easter *Gemeindebildung*, or reflection on the part of the community, with the etiological purpose of explaining the name Peter/Rock and characterizing that apostle's unique function as first witness to the faith in the resurrection, on which the church is built—as also to proclaim the petrine doctrinal authority, and Peter's decision to set out on mission and thus guarantee the future of Christ's church.[19]

This passage must be inserted into the general outlook of the New Testament—not isolated from the context described above. Otherwise it yields not an ecclesiology but a "hierarchiology"—a conceptualization of the church "from the top down" in dissociation from the People of God, a church that will be first and foremost the vessel of sacred power.

The Last Supper: Final Eschatological Sign

The texts that have come down to us on the Last Supper presuppose an already existing community organization and eucharistic praxis.[20] In its primitive meaning, however, the Last Supper appears to have had a distinctly eschatological connotation. The various meals that Jesus is reported to have taken, not only with the disciples but especially with the socially and religiously marginalized, have a salvific-eschatological meaning: God offers salvation to all, invites the good and the evil without distinction into an intimacy with God. The eschatological character of the Last Supper as a symbol of the heavenly repast to be enjoyed in the kingdom of God appears very clearly in the Lucan text. Here we have an event described having no organic connection with the life of the church, but only with Christ, and this favors its authenticity:[21]

"I have greatly desired to eat this Passover with you before I suffer. I tell you, I will not eat again until it is fulfilled in the kingdom of God."

Then taking a cup he offered a blessing in thanks and said: "Take this and divide it among you; I tell you, from now on I will not drink of the fruit of the vine until the coming of the Reign of God. . . . I for my part assign to you the dominion my Father has assigned to me. In my kingdom you will eat and drink at my table, and you will sit on thrones judging the twelve tribes of Israel" [Lk. 22:15–19, 29–30].

The supper here would be the festive anticipation of the kingdom about to burst in upon humankind. The Eucharist, meanwhile, pertains to the total Christological event, which includes not only Jesus' earthly life and activity, but also his resurrection, and the activity of the risen One through his Spirit after Pentecost. Now that mission is under way, and the Parousia is no longer imminent, the Eucharist is linked by the community to the Last Supper, the farewell supper of the Lord, and is taken as community nourishment and sustenance, as symbol of unity and, preeminently, as continuing presence and representation of the Lord's sacrificial offering. In this reflection on and development of the Eucharist, the Eucharist is a constitutive element of the church. Without it the church would not be what it is.

Jesus' Eschatology: At Once Present and Future

The conceptualization of the kingdom of God and the signs of its appearance carry a recognizably eschatological note: "The reign of God is at hand!" (Mk. 1:15).[22] Jesus himself, in his person, message, and demands, is the kingdom-present, the stronger one who exorcises the strong one (Mk. 3:27). The kingdom is in your midst (Lk. 17:21), and ". . . if it is by the finger of God that I cast out devils, then the reign of God is upon you" (Lk. 11:20). At Jesus' word, diseases are healed (Mt. 8:16–17), storms calmed (Mt. 8:27), the dead raised (Mt. 5:39), and demons expelled (Mt. 12:28). Blessed are the men and women who see in Christ's actions the time of salvation (Mt. 13:16; Lk. 10:23).

If the kingdom is present grandeur, it possesses a future dimension as well. The age of the sinful world will be past (Lk. 17:26–30), sufferings will be no more (Mt. 11:5), death will have been vanquished (Lk. 20:36), the last will be first and the first last (Mk. 10:31), and the scattered elect will all be reunited (Lk. 13:27). The irruption is imminent. Jesus shares the expectations of his generation, as three unambiguous passages testify:

Mark 9:1 (cf. parallels): "I assure you, among those standing here there are some who will not taste death until they see the reign of God established in power."

Mark 13:30 (cf. parallels): "I assure you, this generation will not pass away until all these things take place."

Matthew 10:23: "I solemnly assure you, you will not have covered the towns of Israel before the Son of Man comes."

It is God's alone to know and determine the exact hour (Mk. 13:32; Mt. 24:42–44, 50; 25:13). Still we cannot deny the expectation in which Jesus and his whole generation lived. This is not the place to interpret this expectation and its nonrealization within the framework of a sound Christology.[23] In any case, one thing is certain: the message of the kingdom as victory over all the evils stigmatizing the world, and the total fulfillment of all reality in God, constitutes the heart of Jesus' proclamation of joy to all the people (Lk. 2:10).

Death and Resurrection of Christ:
Sine Qua Non for the Existence of the Church

In a way, Jesus "failed" of his intent to inaugurate the reign of God. The Jews were not converted. In fact in one of their politico-religious conflicts they actually crucified Jesus. But in spite of his awareness of his failure (Mk. 15:34), Jesus did not despair. He accepted death for all, and entrusted himself in confidence to God.

God, however, actualized Jesus' expectation. God concretized the kingdom in Jesus' person. In Jesus we have real, concrete victory over all the limitations inherent in our fallen situation of suffering and death. The kingdom of God, which will now be realized universally owing to its rejection on the part of the Jews, has been inaugurated in Jesus alone. His resurrection is confirmation that the kingdom of God is possible, and that the new heavens and a new earth need no longer be utopia. As Origen says, the risen Jesus is the *autobasileia tou Theou*—God's kingdom personalized.

The reign of God finds no universal realization—only a personal one, in Jesus. But this opens up the possibility of a continuation of this realization in history, and of the appearance of what we call "church" as the community that continues to preach the message of the kingdom, the kingdom already realized by anticipation in the risen Christ and all who believe, but still to come eschatologically.

Without Christ's "failure," the church would be out of place and meaningless. The church presupposes Christ's death and resurrection: his death as condition of the possibility of its existence, and his resurrection as the object of a faith that constitutes a primitive community living in that resurrection as the concretization of the kingdom that Jesus preached. The church, then, possesses the distinct character of a replacement for the kingdom. On the one hand, it is the kingdom-present inasmuch as the risen One is present there. On the other hand, it is not the kingdom inasmuch as the latter is still to be realized eschatologically. The church is at the service of the kingdom, is its sacrament, is the sign and instrument of its appearance and realization in the world.

Let us now carry out a more detailed analysis of the conditions of the appearance of the church. In this way we shall be able better to clarify its essence and meaning. Here we shall follow theses already proposed in 1929, by Erik Peterson, quite some time before being taken up by Romano Guardini and carried further by Joseph Ratzinger.[24]

A Church of Jews and Gentiles

To recapitulate: Jesus preached the kingdom of God, not the church. But the kingdom did not come, although Jesus kept wishing to the very end, because the Jews refused conversion, refused acceptance of a kingdom in a non-nationalistic form. Hence Peterson's first thesis: "*The church exists only contingently upon the fact that the Jews, God's chosen people, did not believe in the Lord. It is of the very concept of the church that it is essentially a church of gentiles.*"[25]

The chosen people rejected Jesus, and thus failed as a people, historico-salvifically. While perceiving this rejection, Jesus did not retreat into a sect, but continued to preach the kingdom to the whole people. He accepted death for all human beings, in fidelity to his mission. Now that he could not win human beings with his message and works, he would win them by taking on himself the sins of the world. From this it follows that Christ's community, too, should exercise the function of reconciliation and self-bestowal, as Jesus has done. They will have to be the vehicles of the revolutionary idea of the kingdom of God, and will have to understand their existence as a being-for-others, as Jesus understood his.[26]

That the church is a church of the Gentiles is a fact of enormous hermeneutical relevance. The church will now abandon a Semitic language and mentality, the instruments with which biblical revelation has always been articulated. It will undertake to render a legitimate translation of Christ's message into another understanding of being—the Graeco-Roman. Acculturation, for example this Hellenistic one, is legitimate for Christianity, and pertains to the process of concretization of the church as church of the Gentiles. No longer need the Gentiles become Jews, and pass by way of the pedagogy of the Old Testament. The basic concepts of the Christian message will be projected upon other cultural coordinates, and hence will share in the lot—the losses and gains—of any translation. The existence of the church through the centuries is concrete proof that the Parousia is being delayed.

This brings us to Peterson's second thesis: "*The church exists only contingently upon the fact that the second coming of Christ was not imminent: in other words, that concrete eschatology was suspended and in its place the doctrine of the last end of the human being had entered the picture.*"[27]

The Last Things are not the world's collapse in the face of the arrival of the eschatological kingdom, but the world's transposition into a new situation, even before time comes to an end. Not the Jews, but the Gentiles believed in Jesus. The church sprang up in virtue of the failure of the end of the world to come. It has the right, then, to proclaim Jesus' message, morality, and so on in a language and perspective no longer eschatological but historical, taking account of the variations in the course of times and ages, including those of the future, which is still open. And so Gospel passages that have an immediate eschatological content, like the Sermon on the Mount, can and must be interpreted in an ethical-moral and ascetical sense.

This temporal perspective was not at first understood by the primitive church. The apostles did not found the church immediately after Pentecost. They looked upon themselves as a group of believing Jews, striving to win the whole people for the kingdom and the risen Christ, who they hoped would shortly come on the clouds of his glory.[28] They kept strictly to the words of the historical Jesus: "Do not visit pagan territory and do not enter a Samaritan town. Go instead after the lost sheep of the house of Israel" (Mt. 10:5-6). Mission was yet unthought of. Only the coming of the Son of Man in power, and the pilgrimage of all the peoples of the earth to Mount Zion, was on any Christian's horizon. This eschatological preoccupation of the *Urgemeinde*, the primitive Christian community, may be observed in its concern to reconstitute the symbolic number of the Twelve, in order to continue thereby to symbolize the imminent eschatological restoration of the twelve tribes of Israel.

The resistance of the people, however, the martyrdom of James in the year 42, Peter's imprisonment and flight, even the conversion of Hellenic Gentiles and Cornelius, induced the little community to cease to regard the irruption of the kingdom as imminent, and to turn to the pagans.

Thus we come to Peterson's third thesis: "*The church exists only contingently upon the fact that the twelve apostles, called and inspired by the Holy Spirit, determined to go to the Gentiles.*"[29]

Christ, Bond of Church and Kingdom

A decisive step has been taken. The apostles embarking on mission have concretely founded the church, and it perdures to the present day. They have taken up the elements that the historical Jesus had introduced, translated them for the new situation, and established in the light of the Holy Spirit the basic structures of the church. First, the actual message of Christ concerning the kingdom is translated into a doctrine on the church and the future of the world. The Twelve will now no longer have a purely eschatological function. They will be the twelve apostles, "persons sent" to the Gentiles. As apostles, they now belong to the church, not the kingdom.[30] Thus the book of Revelation (21:14) ranges them among the foundation stones of the heavenly Jerusalem. And now, in a perspective of an organized church, they may actually be called twelve "*apostles*" in Saint Luke or Saint Matthew. Now they are seen as the first Messianic community, seed of the future church community, even in their existence in the time of the pre-Easter Jesus.

The Eucharist will no longer be merely an eschatological sign of the imminence of the kingdom. Now, in the time of the church, it will be the community's nourishment, the place where the People of God, by eating the body of Christ, become the body of Christ. In the Eucharist, Christ's gift of himself to all men and women, is perpetuated, established for all time. It was surely in this ecclesiological perspective that the eucharistic passages of the Gospels as we have them today were developed.

The passage from Israel to the Gentiles is represented in the parable of the king who was giving a wedding feast for his son. Friends had been invited, but had refused the invitation. Beside himself with fury, the king sent his armies to destroy their city. And then he invited the starving persons of the highways and byways to come take the place of the original guest list. Saint Matthew, who recounts this parable, is confronted with the failure of Israel, the destruction of Jerusalem, and the mission to the Gentiles (Mt. 21:1–14; cf. Lk. 14:16–24). The church is the *Ersatz*, the substitute, for the unrealized kingdom. What connects the kingdom with the church is Christ, present in both. Christ provides the basis for a continuity between the two.

A Church Founded by Christ and by Apostles Moved by the Spirit

The origins of the concrete, historical church as Hans Küng says,

> do not lie solely in the intention and the message of Jesus in the pre-Easter period, but in the whole *history of Jesus' life and ministry*: that is, in the entire action of God in Jesus Christ, from Jesus' birth, his ministry and the calling of the disciples, through to his death and resurrection and the sending of the Spirit to the witnesses of his resurrection. . . . It was not any particular words of Jesus, nor ultimately his teachings, but his person as the hidden Messiah and as the risen Christ, which historically speaking constitutes the roots of the Church.[31]

The death and resurrection of Jesus Christ count most in this Christological event. In its essential elements—its message, the Twelve, baptism, the Eucharist—the church was preformed by the historical Jesus. In its *concrete, historical* form, it sprang from the decision of the apostles, as enlightened by the Holy Spirit (cf. Acts 15:28).

Indeed, tradition has always held that the church was born on the day of Pentecost. Thus it could have one foundation in Christ and another in the Spirit. This conception is of great importance, for it testifies to the fact that the charismatic element, from the very beginning, had an institutional character, and was not fortuitous or transitory.

The church-as-institution was not based, as one so often hears, on the incarnation of the Word, but on faith in the power of the apostles, inspired by the Spirit, who enabled them to transfer eschatology to time, the time of the church, and to translate the doctrine of the kingdom of God into the doctrine of the church, that kingdom's imperfect, temporal realization.[32]

If the church was born of a decision of the apostles under the impulse of the Spirit, the power of community decision in the areas of discipline and dogma pertain to the essence of church. If the church itself sprang from a decision, it will continue to live if Christians and men and women of faith in the risen Christ and his Spirit permanently renew this decision, and incarnate, enflesh the church in the new situations with which they are confronted, be it in the Greek and medieval culture of yesterday or in the popular culture of today in Latin America.

The church is still being sent to the Gentiles. The church is not a completely established, definite quantity. It is ever open to new situational and cultural encounters. Within these realities, the church must live and proclaim, in understandable language, the liberating message of the kingdom, already realized in Christ, and to be realized for all men and women at the consummation of the ages.

The Kingdom Comes to Us via the Church

Finally, to be sure, the question is posed that lurks behind all these reflections. *Why* was the kingdom proclaimed if God knew all along that the church would appear instead? *Why* was it Christ's failure that made it possible for the church to exist?

What would have happened if the Jews had believed in Jesus? We do not know, nor is it important for the faith. What is important is the realities that did historically occur, like the message of the kingdom and the existence of the church, which continues to proclaim the kingdom as Christ did.

Saint Paul, in Romans 9–11, poses the problem of the relationship between Israel's faithlessness and the appearance of the church of the Gentiles. He concludes by confessing the mystery of God's incomprehensible plan.[33] The same problem arises when we reflect on the existence of original sin within God's plan. Really and concretely, this involves a certain failure for a determinate design of God. We know that God permits evil because God has the power to draw good from it and to situate the history of liberation within some other possibility for love and salvation. God's plan includes human beings' freedom, which can frustrate some possibilities and condition others.

The existence of the church testifies to a human freedom that can oppose God. It likewise testifies to the new route that God, in mercy and longsuffering, has selected in order to continue proclaiming the kingdom as the absolute meaning of human beings and their world, a kingdom where God will be all in all (1 Cor. 15:28), in the nth degree of glorification and reverence on the part of every creature.

This understanding of the church, arrived at via a historical examination, does not resolve all the problems posed by the texts of the New Testament. Still, we believe that this route is likely to be more fertile for reaching the meaning and essence of the church than the discussion of theses posited long ago by Scholastic theology. The ways of God, in a sound ecclesiology, intersect with the ways of women and men. God triumphs always, bringing the Good News proclaimed by the Son all the way to us (despite the hardening of human hearts) via the church, which arose thanks to sin, and the grace of God.

Consequences for a Possible Ecclesiogenesis

In this view of things, it can be seen that the church is born of the whole, complex Christological event, with the resurrection and the activity of the Holy

Spirit upon the apostles' decision discharging a vital role. Now we better understand the affirmation of our faith that Jesus Christ founded the church. This is a complex assertion, but within the framework of the mediations analyzed, it is a true one.

If we ask ourselves, after all that we have considered, what institutional form Jesus willed for his church, we can reply: Jesus willed, and continues to will, that form for his church which the apostolic community, enlightened by the Holy Spirit and confronted with the urgencies of its concrete situation, decided and in all responsibility assumed. Obviously the episcopate, the priesthood, and other functions are here for good. This is basic. It is perfectly evident that these structures respond to the ever-present needs that communities have—needs for union, universality, and bonding with the great witnesses of the apostolic past. But more important is the style with which one lives these functions within these communities: whether the functionaries are *over* the communities, monopolizing all services and powers, or *within* them, integrating duties instead of accumulating them, respecting the various charisms and leading them to the oneness of one and the same body. This latter style translates the gospel attitude, and is the praxis that Jesus willed for the Messianic community.

The primitive church, in its essential apostolic character, created functions in response to needs or adapted a style already prevailing, as the synagogal concept was adapted in the college of presbyters. Whether or not to maintain past structures was unimportant. To render the risen One and his Spirit present to the world, to make his liberating message of grace, pardon, and unrestricted love heard, to facilitate human beings' response to these calls—these were the primary concerns. To preserve tradition means to do as the first Christians did. They were attentive to the Spirit, to the words of the historical and risen Jesus, and to the pressures of each situation. They created when they thought they should create, they preserved when they thought they should preserve, and in all things they kept uppermost in mind the triumph of the gospel and the conversion of human beings. This same attitude, basically, has always been maintained in the church. The church has been able both to preserve and to adapt all through history. Ever old and ever new, it has never lost its identity. Christ used all available mediations to render himself present, to reach human beings and save them. The church's way ought not to be different.

Today, as we perceive the possibility of a reinvention of the church, reflections like these present themselves and are astonishingly liberating. They oxygenate the theologico-pastoral atmosphere. They prepare us to try the untried. We see, with Pope Paul VI, in the appearance of the basic church communities, the activity of the Holy Spirit.[34] We must stay on the alert to welcome the emergence of a new presence of church in the midst of men and women, with new services and with new tasks and styles for the old, traditional services.

6

Quaestio Disputata II:
The Lay Coordinator and
the Celebration of the Lord's Supper

The following reflections are intended as a theoretical answer to certain concrete problems. They are not, therefore, offered by way of speculation in the interests of (theological) theory, but in the interests of a practice.

Theological Challenges of a Practice of Celebration

We shall begin with certain factual observations, and attempt to grasp the challenges they represent for theology. There is, in the very concrete case of Latin America, and specifically in Brazil, a chronic lack of ministers ordained by the sacrament of order. No short- or medium-term solution is foreseeable. Official statistics have 1.8 priests for every 10,000 of the faithful, and the proportion is dwindling.[1]

In contrast, the basic church communities are multiplying in nearly all Latin American countries, and now they constitute the vast network that is, as the bishops admitted at the Puebla conference, "one of the motives of joy and hope for the church."[2] Rarely do these communities count any ordained ministers among their members. On the other hand, they do enjoy the services of fine lay coordinators, and a remarkable ferment of new ministries. These communities ardently desire to be able to celebrate the Eucharist.

Rightly does Vatican Council II, maintaining sacred tradition, declare: "No Christian community . . . can be built up unless it has its basis and center in the celebration of the most Holy Eucharist."[3] After all, in "the wonderful sacrament of the Eucharist . . . the unity of the Church is both signified and brought about."[4] For "in the sacrament of the Eucharistic bread the unity of all believers who form one body in Christ (cf. 1 Cor. 10:17)" is both expressed and effectuated.[5] This is why the celebration of the Eucharistic Sacrifice should be "the center and culmination of the whole life of the

Christian community."[6] Well did the Lord say, " . . . If you do not eat the flesh of the Son of Man and drink his blood, you have no life in you" (Jn. 6:53), and "Do this . . . as a remembrance of me" (Lk. 22:19; 1 Cor. 11:25). The basic church communities, however, suffer the absence of the eucharistic celebration, owing to the unavailability of ordained ministers. The official praxis whereby a priest can celebrate the Eucharist without the community, but the community cannot celebrate the Eucharist without the priest, continues to prevail in the church.

Meanwhile, many communities suffering from the want of an ordained minister and desirous of a minister's presence, anxious to share in the communion of the Lord's body and blood, and conscious of their union in faith with the church of the local bishop and pastor, come together "with exultant and sincere hearts" (Acts 2:46) to celebrate, under the presidency of the community coordinator, the Lord's Supper. This generally occurs on the greater liturgical feasts, especially on the occasion of a joint meeting of various regional communities. After a day or two of sharing, prayer, reflection on God's word, and discussions on the problems of life, the need spontaneously arises for a special celebration, whereby these people may be able to express their community life and solemnly ratify the joy of such an encounter. And so they celebrate the Lord's Supper. The celebration resembles the canonical, liturgical Mass. There are scriptural readings, followed by a shared reflection by all and an examination of personal life, with an act of repentance and conversion. There is an offering of either the region's most symbolic produce or bread and wine. Then there is the reading of the account of the Last Supper, the praying of the "Our Father," a communion, and a dismissal. Everything is done with songs, and the songs are often composed in the community itself. Presiding over this celebration is a layperson, having no official ecclesiastical commission—unless, of course, a priest is present, in which case it is he who presides. What is achieved by this lay celebration is what Vatican Council II calls the Eucharist as wellspring and bolster of the Christian life and all evangelization.[7]

As the basic communities grow, they themselves provide more and more of the services that meet their needs.[8] The people's awareness that they all are church, and therefore responsible, lends a new urgency to the question: Now that our coordinators perform all the pastoral tasks that an ordained minister performs, why can they not consecrate and absolve? When a theologian comes to visit a basic church community—and here this writer can add personal testimony to that of so many others—questions never fail to be asked: What is the theological value of our celebrations? What is to prevent our coordinator from actually consecrating the sacred species, in the capacity as extraordinary minister of the Eucharist? After all, is Christ not present in this community? Why should the layperson who presides, who exercises a real ministry and a true *diakonia*, not be able to posit the sacramental signs of the obvious de-facto presence of Christ?

Possible Theological Responses

First we must say that we have questions here that challenge not only the theologian, but the whole Christian body, and in a direct way those responsible for the global guidance of the church (the pope, the synods, the bishops' conferences). But on the institutional level we have immobilism and indifference in the face of the eucharistic emergencies of the basic communities. We hear complaints about the growing shortage of priests, and dramatic appeals for celibate vocations, but new avenues arouse fear.

The normal thing for organized communities would be to have these community presidents receive the sacrament of order.[9] However, these coordinators are not celibate. *Factually*, a precept of ecclesiastical discipline—the law of celibacy—is preventing the implementation of a divine precept: "Do this as a remembrance of me," a precept accompanied by the warning, "If you do not . . . you have no life in you." Can the church any longer tolerate such a situation without serious prejudice even to the numerical increase of its membership? There would be good reasons, going back to the most primitive apostolic tradition, for ordaining married men with good family relationships (cf. 1 Tim. 3; Tit. 1:5–9). We are becoming more and more aware, in Latin America, in Africa, and even in Europe and the United States, that to deprive thousands upon thousands of communities of the sacrament of the Eucharist, and of the incomparable benefits of having an ordained minister, through inflexibility in maintaining a tradition that has bound a necessary service (that of priesthood) to a free charism (that of celibacy) is tantamount to an unlawful violation of the rights of the faithful. Immobilism begets makeshift remedies, and pastoral responsibility is the victim. It is no wonder, then, that communities find their own solutions.

For the theologian, if we may be permitted to simplify a bit, the problem admits of two basic solutions: one in the spirit of immobility, the other in creativity. Immobilism will recite the official line: celebrations of the Lord's Supper by lay coordinators are invalid by the simple fact that these coordinators' have not received the sacrament of order.[10] Their celebrations are "sacramentals," but not sacraments; they are paraliturgies at most. They are not simply nothing at all, of course, since they do express the *votum sacramenti* and thus attain the *res*, the grace of the presence of and (spiritual) communion with Christ.

The response of creativity understands that theology's task is not exhausted in the exposition and explication of the official teaching of the church. Theology also has the mission of seeking out adequate answers to new and urgent problems, using the resources of the *depositum fidei*. This "deposit" does not flow exclusively in channels of official doctrine. Nor is it a stagnant cistern. It can run along new paths that, without denying official doctrine, show the real wealth of the Christian "sacrament," the Christian mystery, especially in cases of pressing need. The "deposit of faith" is a spring of living water—water that flows. This is the service for which one looks to theology. It should extract, from its store of treasures, not just the old, but the new as well (cf. Mt. 13:52).

This matter is not limited to those within the Catholic pale. It implies an ecumenical discussion: What is the value of the eucharistic celebrations of the churches issuing from the Reformation, when we know that their ministers have not received the sacrament of order? Catholic reflection has made considerable advances in this area.[11] This can be useful for the question at hand, since what holds for Protestant celebrations should hold a fortiori for the celebrations of Catholic lay coordinators.

Our presentation will be made in three steps. First we shall offer a rapid historical sketch.[12] Then we shall attempt to draw everything we can from the wealth of official doctrine and apply it to the present subject matter. Finally we shall try to focus the question in the light of an adequate ecclesiology, since it is in ecclesiology that the problems and their potential solutions are to be found.

In Ancient Times the One Who Presided also Consecrated

The New Testament gives us nothing certain to go on regarding the presidency of the eucharistic celebration. Acts 13:1–2 and the Pauline letters suggest that the celebrants were simply those who presided in the communities—prophets, teachers, and apostles. According to the Didache, which dates from before the year 100, prophets presided at the Eucharist.[13] Bishops and deacons who are selected to celebrate are assimilated to prophets and teachers.[14] For Clement of Rome (A.D. 95), the ministers of the Eucharist are again those who preside in the community—the bishops and priests.[15] These, however, are not sacerdotal personages for Clement. Ignatius of Antioch (A.D. 110) says reproachfully: "Let that Eucharist be held valid which is offered by the bishop or by one to whom the bishop has committed this charge."[16] His meaning is: the bishop, principle of the unity of the church, is also president at the sacrament of unity, the Eucharist. For Justin (A.D. 150), it is the "one presiding," the "president," the *proestōs*, without any connotation of apostolic succession, who is the celebrant.[17] Hippolytus of Rome, sometime between A.D. 217 and 235, makes it clear that the president of the community is also president at the Eucharist.[18] But he lays down a condition: the bishop, selected by all the people, must receive, by the laying-on of hands of other bishops, the "apostolic charism," together with the "primacy of the priesthood" for the "offering of the oblations of Holy Church."[19] This is the earliest record that we have of a sacerdotal characterization of the celebrant of the Eucharist.

For Tertullian (A.D. 223), it is the *probati seniores*, the attested elders—the "elders tried and true," shall we say—who preside over the church,[20] and it is from their hands alone that we receive the Eucharist,[21] since the sacerdotal functions lie in their charge.[22] Thus for Tertullian there is a special bond between presidency in the community and presidency at the Eucharist. And yet the absence of anyone constituted in the *ecclesiasticus ordo* is no absolute impediment to this celebration. Tertullian explicitly asserts: " . . . Are not we lay people also priests? . . . Hence, where there is no such hierarchy, you yourself offer sacrifice, you baptize, and you are your own priest. Obviously, where there are three gathered together, even though they are lay persons, there is a church."[23] The passage is from Tertullian's Montanist period, but it represents the conceptualization he always maintained of the priesthood. To be sure, he repeatedly insists that one must do this only *ubi necesse est*, "where necessary." Here he takes his distance from the Montanists, who assigned priestly functions to laity without necessity.[24]

A direct attestation of the celebration of the Eucharist by laity comes down to us from Theodoret of Cyr (A.D. 466), in his *Ecclesiastical History*, where he refers to the exhortation received by merchants arriving in Ethiopia "to assemble, according to the custom of the Romans, to take part in the divine liturgy."[25] Saint Cyprian of Carthage (A.D. 258) is the first to attest in writing to the celebration of the Eucharist by presbyters without the presence of the bishop (although never in opposition to him—this would be sacrilege).[26]

Hippolytus, speaking of ordination, says: "Lay not hands upon a confessor for the diaconate or the presbyterate. Truly, the dignity of presbyter equals the honor of his confession. But if he be ordained a bishop, let hand be laid upon him."[27] The "confessor," therefore, the one who has suffered persecution for the faith, may celebrate the Eucharist even without benefit of ordination, simply because he has become a presbyter, or president of the community. The basic rule in ancient Christianity was: *Whoever presides over the community—* be his title bishop, presbyter, prophet, teacher, or confessor—*presides ex officio at the Eucharist as well.*[28]

If we analyze the oldest liturgical prayers—whether that of Hippolytus or those of others—it is sufficiently clear that presidency at the liturgical celebration is an expression of the capital task of mission: presiding in the community.[29] This would explain the renowned Sixth Canon of the Council of Chalcedon, which was considered binding by the whole church up to the twelfth and thirteenth centuries, and is held by the Eastern church even today:

No one shall be ordained at large, either to the presbyterate, or diaconate, or to any place in the ecclesiastical order whatsoever; nor unless the person ordained be particularly designated to some church in a city, or village, or to some martyr's chapel, or monastery. And if any have been ordained without charge, the holy synod has decreed such ordination to be null and nowhere operative, to the reproach of the ordainer.[30]

This bond between the community and those charged with its direction is very strict, we see. This is for a reason: the celebration is never that of the celebrant alone. It is always the celebration of the whole community. This is demonstrated by an analysis of the liturgical vocabulary of the first thousand Christian years. "The priest does not celebrate just by himself, nor does he consecrate just by himself. The whole community of the faithful, who are with him, consecrate and sacrifice with him."[31]

As we shall see below, statements of the magisterium to the effect that the bishop and the priest are the sole ministers of the eucharistic celebration—as reaffirmed, for example, by Innocent III, or the Fourth Lateran Council, or, finally, the Council of Trent—must be understood within, and not apart from, the larger tradition of 1,000 years.[32] *Ordinary* ministers are being talked about here. The priesthood of the faithful cannot be appealed to as the basis of an ordinary ministry paralleling that of the ordained priest. There may be no legitimate ministers "against" the ordinary ministry, as Cyprian would say.

Edward Schillebeeckx, in a remarkable historico-theological study, has traced this problem back through 2,000 years of the celebration of the Lord's parting deed, and finds that the whole first millennium of church history was lived under the sign of a "pneumatological-ecclesial" conceptualization of ministry and of presidency at the eucharistic celebration.[33] Initially, even in the New Testament, "ecclesiastical ministry" is not defined in function of the Eucharist, but in function of the essential apostolicity of the community. It is the preaching, admonition, upbuilding, solidification, and direction of the community that is decisive. Being a minister basically has to do with the direction of the community. Titles are of scant importance. The community has the inalienable right to celebrate the Eucharist: "Do this as a remembrance of me." It does so through and with its president, who is president not simply because he has received his investiture through *ordination*. On the contrary, first he is called and designated by the community (*cheirotonia*). This act is understood by the ancient church as manifestation of the Spirit in the community. This is how the president is inserted into a determinate community. Next, in a liturgical framework, the laying-on of hands is performed (*cheirothesia*), and the "gift of God" is called down upon the one designated. *Ordinatio* implies both the designation and the laying-on of hands. But principally, and as a sine qua non, we recall Chalcedon's Sixth Canon, which implies the designation by the community. By this insertion into the community the president receives all the necessary faculties for the direction of the community, including that of presiding at the eucharistic celebration.[34]

With these premises established, Schillebeeckx continues:

> We may therefore conclude that a situation in which a community was unable to celebrate the Eucharist because there was no bishop or presbyter present was unthinkable in the early Church. As Jerome commented: "No Church community without a leader." On the basis of the right of the community to the Eucharist, the leader of the community also has the right to lead in the Eucharist. The community cannot, moreover, live evangelically without the Eucharist because it is a Eucharistic community, that is, a community that celebrates the Eucharist. If there is no leader, it chooses a suitable candidate from its own ranks. What are involved here are the evangelical identity and the Christian identity of the community.[35]

In the mentality of the church of the first millennium, the president or coordinator of one of our basic communities—the coordinator selected by the community and accepted by the other churches and by the bishop—would have been the natural one to preside at the celebration of the Lord's Supper.

The connections are different in the church today, where the connection is between the ordained priest and the sacrament of the Eucharist. In the ancient church it was between the director and the community. The community had the right to celebrate the Eucharist, and when it did so, someone presided, namely, the director whom that community had officially selected and recognized by the laying-on of hands. This director then concelebrated and coconsecrated with the community. The sacerdotalism of the president came later, as Saints Cyprian and Hippolytus testify. Initially the eucharistic sacrifice was allegorized in terms of the sacrifices of the Old Covenant, with the bishop as the high priest. We should note that it was only the bishop who was allegorized as the priest, for it was he who was normally the director of the community. When, in the course of time, the presbyters too became community directors, and so presided at the Eucharist, then they too gained the title of priest, *secundi meriti*, of second rank, in subordination to the president-bishop.[36] But this incipient sacerdotalism made no change in the basic tone of the whole first 1,000 years, which was founded on the linkage between the community and its director. According to some authors, the director occasionally acquired the title of "priest," along with other titles.

The second millennium, however, unfolded under the sign of a directly Christological and privatizing grounding of ministry. The feudal disputes between *Imperium* and *Sacerdotium*, the consequent growth of a science of canon law that developed a conception of authority as a value in itself without any connection to community (the ontologization of the *sacra potestas*), the need to ensure a means of livelihood for the clergy (resulting in the creation of the *beneficium*), and finally, extratheological and secular considerations—all led to the dislocation of the poles upon which an understanding of the ecclesial ministry had been articulated. Instead of designation/insertion into the community, the laying-on of hands gained the greater value, independently of the community. The "character" of the sacrament of order, for the great medieval theologians, still expressed the nexus between community and minister.[37] However, it began to be ontologized—understood as the means whereby the priest directly participates in the priesthood of Christ and constitutes, ontologically, a specific class of Christian, alongside the simple baptized, or common priests. He can be ordained absolutely, without a bond with any community. Bound directly to Christ, the priest renders Christ present, acquires the *potestas conficiendi corpus Domini*, the power of confecting the Eucharist, of consecrating the sacred species. Even so, privatized as the new concept is, the priest's action is valid only in community, in the sense that he must intend to do what the church does. This conceptualization of ministry is without real ecclesiological foundation. It rests solely on an ontological, privatizing Christology. Vatican Council II sought to strike a compromise between the two great ecclesiological currents of *communio* and of *sacra potestas*, without, however, altering the outlines of the prevailing concept of ministry.

Two thousand years of church history clearly show the importance of the historical factor in the constitution of the various services and the different forms of church authority. The community never stopped being coordinated. There were always directors, whether in a framework of an ecclesiology of consensus (the first millennium) or within the parameters of an ecclesiology of authority (the second millennium). Either way, the order of the community was preserved.

Today we are confronted with practices which, while not *contra ordinem*, are indeed *praeter ordinem*. History has shown us that practices prevailing on the margins of the community order often finish by dynamizing that order, and conferring on it a new ecclesial expression that is later officially assimilated. One wonders, then, whether, along with the ordained ministers of any of the sacraments, there could not be extraordinary ministers as well, with a valid ministry.

When we appreciate that, according to the church's most ancient tradition, "who presides, also consecrates," we open the door to an ecclesiological understanding of celebrations held in communities that are deprived of ordained ministers, and which therefore avail themselves of an extraordinary minister to satisfy their desire for a sacramental presence of the Lord in their midst.

The problem, as we have said, presents its ecumenical face as well. Reflection already in progress in this area may help to reinforce our own argumentation. Here one seeks to understand the celebrations of non-Roman-Catholic Christian churches along two connected avenues: that of the Eucharist, which is de facto being celebrated in the community in question; and that of baptism, with its basic value as gateway to all the other sacraments. Let us apply this approach to the case before us.

The Eucharistic Pole: The Value of the Apostolic Teaching on the Eucharist

We begin with the fact that the churches stemming from the Reformation do actually celebrate the Lord's Supper, bona fide, and today without any anti-Roman animus. Their ministers are accepted by their respective communities as qualified to preside at these celebrations. The validity of the latter is seen as guaranteed by the apostolic succession, but this succession is understood as constituted not only by the laying-on of hands, but by substantial fidelity to the apostolic teaching concerning the presence of the Lord in the celebration of his parting act.

There is a new tendency on the Catholic side to go beyond a juridico-formal understanding of an apostolic succession mediated by the imposition of hands alone and with this laying-on of hands constituting priestly ordination. First, so the new thinking goes, a mechanical imposition of hands is insufficient. Agreement of mind and intention with the teaching of the apostles is presupposed and demanded. *Apostolic succession* is in function of *apostolic teaching*.

Second, apostolicity is not a mark of particular members of the church but of the whole church. There is genuine apostolic succession in the heritage of the apostolic faith, in witness to the Lord who died and rose again, in community service, in mission, in the preferential service of the poor. "It is not apostolic succession which makes the church Catholic, but the catholicity of the Church which guarantees apostolic succession."[38] The transmission of sacramental grace and apostolic succession, therefore, is no longer looked upon as flowing directly from the apostles to the ministers of today, but as flowing via the conformity of today's eucharistic doctrine with that inherited from the apostles and Catholic tradition. What is decisive for sacramental value lies in the acceptance of faith in the Lord present and living in the eucharistic celebration, and in the value of the eucharistic celebration as representation of Christ's sacrifice, and not only of the Last Supper. In this view, the Eucharist celebrated by ministers without any bond with the tradition of the laying-on of hands would be valid and sacramental in virtue of the apostolic doctrine of the real presence of Christ—notwithstanding the absence of the celebrated apostolic succession of the laying-on of hands.

Thus, in the basic communities the celebration of the Lord's Supper would win its validity thanks to the Catholic faith of these communities, by which they experience the conviction that the risen One is truly rendered present in their celebrations.

The Baptismal Pole: The Whole Church as Priestly

Another solution is attempted along the lines of an appeal to an adequate appreciation of baptism. Because baptism is the sacrament of initiation par excellence, it must somehow contain all the wealth of mystery and sacrament. By baptism an entire people becomes priestly. The sacrament of order is not the sacrament of the bishop or priest; it is a sacrament of faith and a sacrament of the church. The priestly ministry (of bishop or priest), therefore, even if it enjoys a difference from the universal priesthood that is not just of degree but also of kind, is nevertheless part and parcel of the one priesthood of Christ. It exists for the benefit of all the priestly people of God. According to Thomistic theology, baptism itself contains and implies a *votum* of the Eucharist, which consummates the "communion" intended by baptism. Normally the community is provided with ordinary ministers to preside over it in all respects—in faith, in charity, in leadership—and in its celebrations. But extraordinary situations can occur, as with the divisions that took place in the sixteenth century.

For extraordinary situations could there not perchance be extraordinary ministers? The history of the sacraments shows us that for all or nearly all of the sacraments there are extraordinary ministers: for baptism, confirmation, marriage, the sacrament of the sick, and reconciliation (administered by laity). Could there be such for the Eucharist? The history to which we refer shows us that, initially, the ordinary ministers of the sacraments were the bishops, as presidents of their respective communities, but that they could entrust others with the responsibility. The anti-Donatist Council of Arles (314) promulgated this canon: "We enjoin deacons, who we know celebrate the Eucharist in many places, to restrict those celebrations as much as may be possible."[39] During the persecution of Diocletian (303–11), deacons probably took the place of presbyters and bishops in the celebration of the Eucharist. We know too that popes Boniface IX, Martin V, and Innocent VIII delegated to abbots the power of conferring "all orders," as extraordinary ministers.[40] Thus the possibility of an extraordinary minister for the Eucharist scarcely seems out of the question. The absence of an ordained minister, in the presence of a need and desire for the Eucharist, does not seem to constitute an absolute obstacle to the eucharistic celebration. The common priesthood of the faithful would permit the president of the community to render visible—sacramental—the priestly, eucharistic action of Christ. Thus both the ministers of the churches of the Reformation and basic community coordinators, acknowledged as principle of community unity, would truly celebrate the Lord's Supper. Christ would therefore be sacramentally present.

There are degrees of density of presence, depending on the levels of realization of the sacramental density of the church itself.[41] The sacramentality of the church is not monolithic or homogeneous. The church may experience divisions and breaches in its unity, even in its teaching and its charity. The Eucharist, the sacrament of unity (unity achieved, and ever to be achieved), shares in these various degrees. Only in the eschaton will this sacrament be full, with the fullness that expresses the transparency of Christ in his priestly community. In the absence of an ordained minister, this sacrament is incomplete. Yet the presence of Christ will be genuine, even though it will not be *sacramentally* full.

So far, then, the extraordinary situation. But what if, as in Latin America, the extraordinary becomes ordinary, normal, regular? May communities resign themselves to an ongoing state of deprivation of the greatest sacrament of our faith? If a community already initiated into the Christian mystery, and living in communion with the other communities of the church, has an earnest desire for the sacramental presence of Christ, and not only for the eucharistic grace in virtue of a *votum eucharistiae,* what is this community to be told? Must theology recite the classic formula and deny it the right to share these celebrations? This writer believes that theology holds a store of possibilities springing from a more adequate ecclesiology, an ecclesiology based on communion rather than on sacred power. This ecclesiology of communion, with its explanation of the various distinct ministries or services, in our grave crisis of the ministry today, is being called upon and enjoined to yield all the fruit it can.

The Coordinator as Extraordinary Minister of the Lord's Supper

Basically it is a matter of recognizing the extraordinary situation that calls for an extraordinary solution: the appearance of an extraordinary minister of the celebration of the Lord's Supper. Need knows no law; yet this does not *ipso facto* generate anarchy. It opens the way for forces of church life, and the dynamism of the Spirit pervading the Christian community, to find other expressions. The *ordo caritatis* and solicitude for the *salus animarum* are at the basis of juridical systems in the church. These systems do not exhaust the potential residing in the deposit of the living faith. It is in virtue of this principle and perspective, ever present in the history of the church, that we hear of a theology of the *supplet ecclesia,* the *oeconomia salutis,* and the extraordinary minister.[42]

It is absolutely necessary to begin with an adequate ecclesiology. Instead of taking our point of departure in powers transmitted, as does a juridico-formal conceptualization of the apostolic succession, we must begin with the faith community, in which the Spirit acts, calling forth various services and charisms and directing them unto good. This is a different rationale of articulation: instead of a historical reference to the past, via a linear succession, we have a reference to the presence today of the risen One and his Spirit in the midst of the community, upbuilding it continuously as a community of disciples. This community, whole and entire, is a fundamental sacrament. Whole and entire, it is priestly, and directly priestly—the mediation of ordained minister aside—just by the fact of its faith and its baptism. Thus the faithful are grafted onto Christ, and Christ with all his powers becomes present and active in the community. After all, faith and baptism constitute the minimum reality of church, that sacrament of universal salvation. The task of being sign and instrument—sacrament—of Christ's victory, and of actualizing that victory in all of life's dimensions, belongs to the whole church, not just to certain of its members. Not all are apostles, not all are prophets, not all are teachers (cf. 1 Cor. 12:4, 28), but each receives his or her particular function from God (cf. 1 Cor. 7:7), each for the good of all (cf. 1 Cor. 12:7). All bear witness, all are responsible for truth and oneness, all pray, all participate in the ministry of reconciliation (cf. 2 Cor. 5:18–20). The faithful do not have the charge of direction of the community ex officio, but neither do they cease to be coresponsible for unity. They too offer the Eucharist, and celebrate, and constitute with their ministers the integral subject of the liturgical action.

Initially, therefore, there is no dichotomy between the faithful without any ecclesiological powers and the ordained minister with a fullness of divine power. What we have is a profoundly priestly, prophetic, and real community organized internally, that is, it makes hierarchical and institutionalizes its functions. Each sacrament, in turn, details and concretizes, for various community situations, the primordial sacrament that is the church. The sacraments cannot be taken in themselves, like atoms charged with salvific energy that other acts do not possess. They are concrete expressions of the primordial sacrament that is church. This holds for the sacrament of order, too: the church, priestly in its entirety, specifies this sacerdotal function by conferring on it, through a special rite, a public, official character, and by ordaining, for the good of the whole community, the one called by the Spirit. Order does not, therefore, confer anything exclusive without which the church would be essentially deprived. The relationship is the other way around: the sacrament of order is the explicit, public, organized, and official expression of the charism of unity and of presidency, of which the church community is the permanent vessel. In virtue of the fact that the ordained minister officially expresses the priestly dimension of all the people, the presidency of celebrations of the Eucharist falls to the ordained minister.

What does the sacrament of order specifically confer? It confers ex officio the direction of the community in the name of Christ. This implies that the ordained minister, whose direction of the community includes the direction of its liturgical life, acts "in persona Christi Capitis."[43] It also implies that, with respect to the sacraments, this ordained minister holds the *potestas conficiendi*. But everything depends on how this power is to be understood. Certainly it cannot constitute a power in competition with the definitive, eschatological priesthood of Jesus Christ, the unique Mediator. Now that Christ is come, there can never be priesthood *titulo proprio* other than his. There can be only a priesthood representative of his unique priesthood. Christ is present but invisible. He is not sacramental. The Christian minister (in the original sense of the word "minister") lends visibility (with all that this implies in a celebration) to the priestly ministry of Christ. Christ consecrates, baptizes, and forgives through the intermediary of the ordained minister, who has received the power to celebrate publicly, in the name of Christ and the community, the sacrament. The sacrament of the presbyterate is not, properly speaking, a power to consecrate—this power belongs to Christ—but a power (*the potestas conficiendi*) to represent *really* the power to consecrate that is Christ's.

The service of sacramentalizing Christ in the church is the ordinary function of the ordained minister. Now the question arises: Is this function that of this minister exclusively? Or, in case of need, such as that of a prolonged absence of the latter, without fault on the community's part, could the community coordinator, recognized as such, act as *extraordinary minister*? We hold that there are sufficiently certain theological data, taking into consideration the praxis of the ancient church that the one who presides in the community also presides in the liturgical celebration, to propose the following hypothesis:[44]

1. A community in need, according to "right doctrine," is especially close to the Eucharist, in virtue of faith and the apostolic succession.

2. The entire community, in virtue of faith and baptism, is constituted a priestly community. Here Christ is present, exercising his priestly ministry.

3. The entire community is sacrament of universal salvation, in its capacity as the local presence of the church universal.

4. Through its coordinators, the community is in communion with all its fellow churches and with the church universal. These fellow churches, and the church universal, recognize the *diakonia* of the coordinators.

5. The community is ardently desirous of the Eucharist.

6. The community has been deprived of the Eucharist for a long time, irremediably, without fault of its own, and without having expelled its minister.

7. This community, in virtue of all the above, already has access, through the *votum sacramenti*, to the eucharistic grace (*res*).

8. If this community delegates to its president the presidency in the celebration of the Lord's Supper, then it has the sacramental sign as well as the eucharistic grace (*sacramentum*, hence *res et sacramentum*).

9. This community would therefore celebrate, truly, really, and sacramentally, the Lord's Supper, *praeter ordinem* but not *contra ordinem* or *contra ecclesiam*, in the good faith of confecting that which, in all churches, the ordinary minister confects. Christ, present in the community but invisible, would through the person of the nonordained coordinator, be rendered sacramentally visible.

10. The sacrament, however, even with the High Priest thus present sacramentally, would be *incomplete*, since it is confected *extra ordinem*—the coordinator would be lacking constitution in order, would be lacking ordination in the sacred priestly ministry. The church, root sacrament of all the other sacraments, by *oeconomia* (by the *supplet ecclesia*), would render the liturgical celebration of the community so gathered, the local expression of the universal church, sacramentally valid.

11. The nonordained celebrant would thus be the extraordinary minister of the sacrament of the Eucharist. This minister, qua extraordinary, would always be minister ad hoc, and would never constitute the basis for an ordinary praxis, and therefore not constitute the subject of a ministry in competition with that of the ordinary minister, who is ordained to the sacrament of order.[45]

12. This community celebration ought not to be called the Mass, since the Mass is a rigorously defined reality, theologically, liturgically, and canonically. It could be called the celebration of the Lord's Supper, however, as it would have a ritual organized by the community itself, in which would clearly appear the memorial character of meal, sacrifice, and eucharistic presence of Christ. In this fashion, confusion would be avoided, and the certainty would abide that the Lord, already present in the community, was making even more closely felt his ineffable presence in the rite of the celebration of his Last Supper. Once again the precept would be fulfilled: "Do this as a remembrance of me."

Appendix: Celebration of the Lord's Supper in a Basic Community

Here we append the rite of celebration of the Lord's Supper as actually held in a basic church community in the interior of Brazil on a Holy Thursday. The text was composed by a diocesan pastoral team and distributed to all the basic communities of the diocese in accordance with standard procedure for the liturgical/catechetical assistance provided by this diocese. It was in celebrations like these that we conceived the idea of writing the study we have presented in this chapter.

1. *Preparation of the Place of Celebration*: The place of celebration should be decorated with flowers, in token of festivity. In the center of the space, on a

table or on the ground covered with a tablecloth, place everything that has been brought for the meal. A tea, or other refreshing drink, is to be prepared. At one end of the table, on a plate, place a cake of sweet cassava (manioc or tapioca), and a quantity of assai, cherimoya fruit, cashew nuts, or passion fruit.

2. *Meaning of the Gathering*: Jesus loved his own, and loved them to the very end. He knew that the plan to kill him was about to be carried out. Now he gives the great law of his message: to love as he has loved. And he leaves a sign of this love here among human beings: the Eucharist, the Mass. This is what the group is about to recall and experience this day. Today is a festival day. This is why the meeting place is decorated. The meal in the center is for the purpose of recalling, in a more visible way, Jesus' Last Supper, and the powerfully felt communion of the group that is his.

3. *Celebration*: The monitor should explain that the community is about to re-experience what Jesus did, by means of food and drink familiar to the people and produced in their own region.

Then follow a song of oneness and fellowship, and a prayer of gratitude and praise.

The plate with the cassava or tapioca cake is placed before the eldest person, or a person selected by the monitor, or the monitor. This person then takes up the cake, breaks it, recites or paraphrases Jesus' words as found in Matthew 26:26—"Take this and eat it. . . . This is my body"—and gives a portion to each person present.

All eat of this cake in silence and with great reverence. This is a sacred ceremony, recalling what Jesus did. All pause for a moment, prolonging the silence.

After all have partaken, the same person who distributed the cake takes up the fruit drink and repeats the words of Matthew 26:27–29: "All of you must drink from it, . . . for this is my blood, the blood of the covenant, to be poured out in behalf of many for the forgiveness of sins."

The drink is now distributed in glasses or mugs, a portion to each person present. Once more, this is done in silence, and with reverence.

After another moment of silence, there may be singing. The songs selected should be appropriate for the occasion of this special act: for example, "Os cristãos tinham tudo em comun" ["Christians held all things in common"], or some other song of oneness and unity.

4. *Commitment of Service*: After the ceremony of the meal is ended, the next ceremony begins, recalling Jesus' sign of service—his washing of the feet of his disciples. Today all are to do as he did.

There is a song of mutual help and service, followed by a reading from the Gospel of John (13:1–17). The reading may be dramatized if those present so desire.

Someone previously designated now offers a brief commentary explaining that all should do what Jesus did: serve their fellow Christians and help everyone. The explanation should end with a statement to the effect that some persons in this group or community are specially designated to serve the community in various ways: coordinators, monitors, catechists, ministers of the sick, ministers of marriage, and so on. The names of all who perform these official community services are mentioned.

All rise.

The monitor, the catechist, and anyone else who performs an official service in the community makes a commitment, in his or her own words, to continue working for the community in the service of his or her sisters and brothers. Those present may ask questions, and those with a community service should respond.

When the ministers have finished speaking, they kneel while the others, standing, lift their hands in the direction of those kneeling and sing an invocation to the Holy Spirit (such as "A nós descei divina luz" ["Descend to us, O light divine"] or "Derrama Senhor" ["Pour out, O Lord"], or another), repeating it two or three times.

Finally, all pray the "Our Father," with arms uplifted.

The monitor, the coordinator, and other persons who have made commitments of service in the community begin to serve those present at the meal with the aliments that have been brought and are waiting on the table, or on the tablecloth on the ground. All joyfully share the repast, in a spirit of solidarity.

7

Quaestio Disputata III:
Women's Priesthood
and Its Possibilities

Women's Priesthood in a Perspective of Women's Liberation

The basic church communities constitute a privileged locus not only of the Christian freedom of the laity, but of the liberation of woman, as well. More and more in the basic communities, women are assuming functions of leadership. In this context, the problem of women's priesthood arises. In view of the frequency of its broaching, in basic communities as well as outside, we offer the following theological reflection.

The subject of women's priesthood is part of the general subject of women's liberation. Today's world, in varying degrees, but at least in some degree everywhere, is characterized by a broadening of the field of individual liberties—along with the danger of a simultaneous amplification of the potential for the strangulation of this same area of liberty. After many millennia of a patriarchal primacy, the present age is host to a notable change of awareness with respect to the relationships between man and woman and the roles they play in human society.

People generally wish that the difference between the sexes could be acknowledged in a way that would not involve particular privileges for either. The tendency of our planetary civilization is to overcome patriarchalism and matriarchalism and move in the direction of a society of free persons, freely associated in marriage, and independent when it comes to personal fulfillment, with respect for the differences between the sexes, and with every person enjoying the right to live in conformity with this difference. Indeed, we are beginning to see a special human richness residing precisely in the actualization of what is different with each sex, understanding this differential in reciprocity and mutuality. What is being sought is equality in difference.

Any authority enjoyed by either member of the human couple with respect to the other is exercised in a framework of personal equality, and understood not so much as the function of one of the sexes—this concept having been due to the matriarchate or the patriarchate, depending on the case—but as a function freely accepted by both partners, and liable to be exercised now by one, now by the other.

As this tendency gains momentum, woman becomes gradually more liberated from the injunctions of the patriarchal culture to which we have fallen heir. She is passing from a historical function in which she was confined. She is passing from sexual object to person.

Woman had not been understood in function of herself, but in function of man and of the social role he required of her. Socially, woman was identified by her sex, while man was identified by his profession or social function.[1]

The current change of consciousness in the relationship between the sexes tends to permit the emergence of woman as person. Woman's sex continues to perform its function, but it is no longer the exclusive determinant of one's identity. It takes its place in the vaster context of personalization.

This increasingly consistent awareness of woman as a person, and of the equality of the sexes before God, seems to be leading, slowly but surely, to the end of a humiliating, time-out-of-mind "minority of age" for women.[2]

In this liberation process, nascent Christianity was a decisive factor, preaching that for God there is no discrimination among persons, and that, therefore, "there does not exist . . . male or female. All are one in Christ Jesus" (Gal. 3:28). Jesus Christ himself took up woman's defense against arbitrary Judaic marriage legislation. There is a radical equality between man and woman. They are in the image and likeness of God (Gen. 1:27) together, not separately.

However it may be that in its theological intention Christianity contains the germ of a complete liberation of woman from the discrimination of a patriarchal culture that prevailed until recently, in its concrete incarnation Christianity came to adhere to the discriminatory social structures of a Greco-Roman and Judaic culture, and has permitted their continuation within church structures to our very day. Saint Paul himself prescribed the submission of woman to her husband in the same way that the church is subject to Christ (Eph. 5:22–23), using an analogy that we find difficult to accept in our own day.

Canon law, in the 1918 Code, legislates an inferior condition for women in the church. Canon 118 declares women incapable of holding or exercising ecclesiastical office requiring the power of order or jurisdiction. They are simply incapable of priesthood. Consequently they are excluded from all service at the altar, and forbidden even to approach the altar during the celebration of Mass or other liturgical actions (canon 813). It is recommended that women be separated from men in church, and that they keep their heads covered (canon 1267). They are not permitted to administer the sacrament of baptism in danger of death if a man is present to do so (canon 742). Except in case of necessity, they may not confess outside a confessional (canon 910). They may not act in causes of beatification or canonization (canon 2004). They have no right to preach (canon 1327). They may not administer parish property (canon 1521). A married woman necessarily has her husband's domicile (canon 93). And so on.

Since Vatican Council II, these inequalities are tending to disappear. Thus, for example, women are permitted a more ample participation in the liturgy. In Brazil, especially, religious women perform a genuine *diakonia*, liturgical, catechetical, charitable (as social workers in the community), and even pastoral, assuming all parish responsibilities formerly reserved to the priest except the saying of Mass and the hearing of confessions.[3] Many women also work in official or consultative capacities in the various organs of the central government of the Catholic Church in Rome.[4]

How far will the church go here? Will it, can it go all the way to complete equality of opportunity for both sexes with regard to access to the sacred ministry, including admittance to the priesthood? Or will there be structures of so-called divine law and order that will prevent this? Nowadays we hear all sorts of declarations on the part of women's organizations in favor of ordination of women.[5] We hear the same from individuals with a professional interest: "If God loves women as much as men," asked a Fairleigh Dickinson (New Jersey) professor of the sociology of religion in a recent interview, "why does the church reserve its ministries and higher responsibilities to men?" And a Brazilian theologian commented: "A woman can conceive a priest, physically and spiritually: her motherly example can one day result in her child's becoming a bishop. But she herself can never be a priest or a bishop."[6] What good will it do to have a theological theory of women's liberation (cf. Gal. 3:28) if oppressive practices persist in the church?

The theological debate flared up in the 1960s. Opinion remains sharply divided. A significant number of theologians—precisely the best, one sees—no longer consider the traditional argument for the exclusion of women from the hierarchy or order in the church to be a convincing one. Others still hold to the traditional argument, especially in view of certain texts of the New Testament and the constant tradition of the church.

Echoes of this discussion, and a forthright declaration in favor of women's priesthood, were heard in the first Synod of Bishops in Rome, via an intervention of Canadian Cardinal George B. Flahiff. Succinctly but precisely, Flahiff summarized the argument of the traditional theological current in this way:

The classic response, when this question was posed twenty years ago, was:

a) Christ was a man, not a woman.

b) He chose twelve men to be his first pastors, and no woman was among them.

c) Saint Paul expressly declares that women must keep silent in church; hence they could not be ministers of the word (1 Cor. 14:34–35).

d) Paul likewise says that, inasmuch as it was woman who first sinned in Eden, she can have no authority over man (1 Tim. 2:12–15).

e) The primitive church had women ministers, and this continued, especially in the East, up to the sixth century; but these ministers were not ordained. We must conclude that the ministry is an occupation for men only. Let women be content with the lot of the Blessed Virgin and the other women around Jesus: to be faithful and devoted handmaidens.[7]

Cardinal Flahiff concluded that *this historical "proof" can today no longer be considered valid.* He then relayed to the synod the appeal that had come from Canadian women, as endorsed by the Canadian episcopate:

That a representative of the Canadian Catholic Conference urge the forthcoming Synod of Bishops to recommend to the Holy Father the immediate establishment of a mixed commission (that is, composed of bishops, priests, laymen and laywomen, religious men and religious women), to study in depth the question of the ministries of women in the church.[8]

In response to Cardinal Flahiff's appeal, the Holy See, on May 3, 1973, created a commission for the study of "women's mission in Church and society."[9] Shortly afterward, however, the limits of this study were outlined in a special memorandum, which read in part: "The possibility of woman's sacred Ordination is to be excluded from the study from the very outset."[10] Upon what does this ecclesiastical measure rest? On the traditional, dogmatic argumentation? Or merely on a supposed untimeliness or inappropriateness of women's ordination, which would be a pastoral and disciplinary consideration?

Jesus: A Man Speaks Up for Women

We shall here attempt to subject the classical argumentation, as outlined by Cardinal Flahiff, to a critical analysis. Then we shall attempt to resituate the problem in a broader perspective of the mission of the church and the sense of its ministries. First, however, it will be in order to recall the attitude of Jesus toward the women of his time. Jesus' attitude will provide a permanent critique of the church, or any other institution, were it to happen to persist in its discrimination against women merely by reason of the fact that they are women.

If by "feminism" we understand whatever defends the basic equality of women to men, maintains that women are human persons, and opposes any institutions that seek to reduce them to the status of objects, then Jesus Christ was certainly a feminist.[11] After all, the general tenor of his ethical preaching consisted in the liberation of human beings from a legalistic, discriminatory morality, in favor of a morality of decision, freedom, and a communion of sisters and brothers. Just as God makes no distinction among persons, but loves them all (cf. Mt. 5:45), so neither should human beings entertain any "preference of persons." Human beings ought to love all other human beings, without distinction and indiscriminately, as sons and daughters of God and therefore brothers and sisters of one another. This ethical revolution launched by Jesus created a space for the liberation of woman as a person.

Jesus' attitude is electrifying if we compare it with that of ancient Jewish society, in which woman was inferior to man in all things.[12] She was treated as a minor, even if she were married or widowed. Obviously she could not be circumcised, and therefore she was excluded from the Abrahamic Covenant. The Decalogue itself seems to be addressed exclusively to males, and lists women among a husband's chattels (Exod. 20:17).[13] In the synagogues, women kept to a special place, behind gratings or in a women's gallery. They might neither read, nor speak, nor comment on the Torah. A woman had no legal credibility as a courtroom witness; she could not teach children; she could not even pray at table. She was forbidden to study the law, the Pentateuch: "The man who teaches his daughter the Torah teaches her extravagance," or, as we may translate, teaches her to abuse it.[14] "May the words of the Torah be burned, they should not be handed over to women."[15] According to rabbinical theology, a Jew ought to render daily thanks to God for three things: that he is not a Gentile, not a woman, and not ignorant of the law.[16] A menstruating woman was unclean, impure, as was anything she used or even touched. A woman could not appear in public or, especially, follow after and listen to the rabbis. Even her own husband was not to speak to her in the presence of anyone outside the family.

How does Jesus behave in the face of this oppressive, discriminatory tradition? His attitude delivers human beings from the burden of their own past. It opens up a vista of brotherly and sisterly reconciliation and communion. Jesus permits a group of Galilean women to follow him (Lk. 8:1–3; 23:49; 24:6–10; Mt. 17:55–56; Mk. 15:40; Jn. 19:25). Luke knows some of them by name, like Mary Magdalene, Joanna the wife of Herod's steward Chuza, and Susanna. But there were "many others" as well (Lk. 8:1–3). Scandalize his disciples though he might, Jesus paused to converse with a heretic, a Samaritan, a woman who had had five husbands (Jn. 4:27). In Magdalene, the great sinner who bathed his feet with her tears and anointed them with precious oils, he saw not primarily the fallen one, the prostitute, but a human creature to be welcomed and forgiven, against all the Pharisaic and religious good sense of the Simons of then and today (Lk. 7:36–50).

With the adultress of John 7:53–8:11, as Saint Augustine said, misery and mercy met, and mercy triumphed. Instead of looking on this woman as a sex object, Jesus saw in her a person who had fallen, and who could be helped, not just sentenced and stoned. Many were the women helped and healed by Christ, as he demonstrated his sovereignty over social taboos. He healed Peter's mother-in-law (Mt. 8:14–15; Mk. 1:29–31; Lk. 4:38–39), the son of the disconsolate widow of Nain (Lk. 7:11–17), the daughter of Jairus, raising her from the dead (Mt. 9:18–26; Mk. 5:21–43; Lk. 8:40–56), the woman hunched and crippled for eighteen years (Lk. 13:10–17), the Canaanite pagan, to whom he said in astonishment, "Woman, you have great faith!" (Mt. 15:21–28; Mk. 7:24–30), and the woman who had suffered for twelve years from a flow of blood, so that she had been ritually impure and a social outcaste during all that time (Mt. 9:20–22; Mk. 5:25–35; Lk. 8:34–48). Despite all the laws of purification, despite all taboos concerning women—especially sick women—Jesus heals her, and in public. In many of Jesus' parables and other figures, women appear in principal roles (Mt. 12:41–42, cf. Lk. 11:31–32; Mt. 13:33; Mt. 22:23–33, cf. Lk. 20:27–40; Mt. 24: 40–41; Mt. 25: 1–13; Lk. 4:25–27; Lk. 15: 8–10; Lk. 18:1–8; Lk. 21:1–4). Nowhere is a woman presented in the discriminatory clichés of the time. Jesus' attitude toward Martha and Mary is astonishing (Lk. 10:38–42; Jn. 11:1–12). Something an orthodox rabbi would never do, Jesus does in all simplicity: he explains theology to a woman, who sits at his feet like a disciple at the feet of a master (Lk. 10:39).

In all these passages, women appear as persons—as daughters of God and therefore deserving of a respect and love equal to that accorded the rest of humankind. This comes through loud and clear in the passage recounting the day that someone in the crowd, filled with enthusiasm, called to Jesus: "Blest is the womb that bore you and the breasts that nursed you!" Here, woman is sex and mother. Jesus' retort lays bare his mentality. Woman is first of all a person: " 'Rather,' he replied, 'blest are they who hear the word of God and keep it' " (Lk. 11:27–28; cf. Mt. 12:46–50; Mk. 3:31–35; Lk. 8:19–21). A human being is a person to the extent that he or she can hear the word that comes from both the other and the Other, and so live in an existential dialogue.

Quite the opposite of being discriminatory, Jesus' attitude toward women shows his reverence for their equality and dignity. Will the church be able to live up to the stature of its divine Founder and receive from him the critical yardstick for its own understanding of woman? In a world where woman is discovering her identity, can the church be a factor for liberation? Or will it supply the ideological substrate for the legitimation of situations that depersonalize women?

In the light of these questions, let us proceed to an analysis of the classic argument against women's access to sacred orders.[17]

Disciplinary Prescriptions, Not Theological Arguments

In arguments against women's ordination, theology has often used "proof from Scripture" with very little attention to context. This uncritical approach to the question of women's priesthood began with the fait accompli of a ministerial priesthood reserved to men alone, and went on from there. The fact has been taken as an unquestionable given; then, in the light of this given, one proceeded to an ideological intepretation of sacred tradition and a tendentious reading of Scripture passages. We find this true today, even on the part of well-known theologians.[18] Simple recourse to what Scripture and tradition say is insufficient. We have a hermeneutical problem here. How are we to read Scripture and tradition? Do they seek to establish a dogmatic fact, one of divine right, or are they indebted to a cultural and theological context in this matter? Do they express, adequately, Christian positivity for the whole rest of the course of history, or are they merely a temporal-circumstantial incarnation of the major fact of the Christian message concerning equality, a communion of sisters and brothers, and the transcendence of all depersonalizing divisions among human beings in God's name?

The Christian message is not exhausted in any historical articulation. It will always be limited in that articulation, and therefore always able to be transcended, enriched, and corrected. The church itself recognizes that women's claim to de-jure and de-facto parity with men is one of the signs of today's times.[19] Cannot, indeed must not, this constitute a new hermeneutical locus that will permit us a critical evaluation of the past and its limits? Taking advantage of this hermeneutical opportunity, we now propose to analyze the classic argumentation as defended today in certain theological circles. There are four main points.

First: Jesus Christ was male, not female (an objection appealing to fidelity to history).

By reserving the priesthood to men alone, we are told, the church is giving concrete recognition to the fact that their priesthood comes to them from Jesus Christ, who, historically, was an altogether concrete human being, and who had a sex. The male priest acts *in persona Christi*, representing, in the sacramental visibility of the church, Christ the Head: that is, the concrete person of Jesus Christ, the source of our salvation.

Sed contra: it is a matter of historical contingency only that Jesus Christ was a male. Jesus himself made no theological principle of it. Indeed, nowhere does he lay any emphasis on this difference whatsoever. The case is, rather, the contrary. In all his preaching activities, what Jesus stressed was the transcendence of all divisions among human beings. Indeed he expressly excluded the biological, sexual factor as meaningful in the determination of the new person: "Who is my mother? Who are my brothers? . . . Whoever does the will of my heavenly father is brother and sister and mother to me" (Mt. 12:48–50).

Saint John well understood the novelty of a Christianity that made men and women sons and daughters of God: "Any who did accept him he empowered to become children of God" (Jn. 1:12). Here the evangelist completely transcends Judaism as a religion based on race. Surely Christianity itself will not be able to tolerate, as a dogmatic principle, the sexual factor as a determinant of eligibility for ministry.

With Christ is inaugurated a new solidarity among human beings, by virtue of which "there does not exist . . . Jew or Greek, slave or freeman, male or female" (Gal. 3:28). To appeal to Christ's maleness in order to justify the privilege of the male sacerdotal ministry is to argue from biology, and thereby to abandon any historical fidelity to Jesus. This is not the legitimate level of argumentation in this area. If such an argument were valid, then why should not priests have to be not only male (since Jesus was a male), but Jewish (since Jesus was Jewish) and indeed, Galilean? Why did the New Testament, which was written in Greek, and why did the church, which officially spoke Greek, then Latin, and today all the languages of the world, not maintain a historical fidelity to Aramaic, the language spoken by Jesus? Why did the church break free of the customs of Judaism, which was the religion and culture of the historical Jesus? This argument from historical fidelity raises more problems than it solves.

A person "represents Christ" not in virtue of factors of flesh and blood, but in virtue of the "faith dimension"—adherence to Christ and his church. That until today men alone have had access to the priestly ministry in the church is due not to the fact that Christ was male, but to factors of a historical and sociological order.

Second: For his apostles Jesus Christ chose men only, not women.

Does the fact that Jesus chose only male apostles mean that it was his explicit will—and therefore of divine law—that no woman have apostolic authority, and therefore that no woman was capable of exercising the priestly ministry? There is no evidence that it did, either in Jesus' message or in the kerygma of the primitive church. Priesthood and official apostolate constitute a social function.

The concretization of this function varies according to variations in society and the cultural situation. From the considerations we have entertained above, it can be seen that, although Jesus may have won all liberties for women in principle, it was simply impossible for a woman to discharge a religio-social function. As Ambrosiaster, the otherwise unknown author of a commentary on thirteen letters of Paul, argued in the fourth century: "In Jesus' time there was no woman prepared for this."[20] If women knew nothing of the law, how could they explain it? They could not appear in public, or come to the synagogue with full rights; how could they exercise a social and religious function?

It is not difficult to understand why Jesus and the apostles did not involve women in the witness to the resurrection, or therefore in the apostolic college. Nor are women cited as witnesses to the apparitions of the risen Lord in 1 Corinthians 15, the oldest written account we have of the resurrection, while the Gospels, which were written later, do mention them. Their testimony simply would not have been accepted. Women were deprived of any juridical qualification whatsoever. It is not a question of the primitive Christian religio-social status of women here. The question is: Given the conditions that actually prevailed, *who could officially represent Jesus Christ and his cause in this concrete cultural situation*?

The answer: Men only. But this does not mean that Jesus and the primitive church were establishing this as a matter of principle forever more, irreformably and definitively. To reason in this fashion would be to sin against the most elementary law of hermeneutics, by detaching sentences and situations from their living context—the socioreligious culture of the time—and absolutizing them.

But, someone will insist, it was to the apostles, at the Last Supper, that Jesus said, "Do this as a remembrance of me." He included no women among the addressees of this precept. Here we must ask: Was Christ concerned only with consecrating the sacred species? Or was he asking for the celebration of the remembrance of his sacrificial death, including eating, drinking, praying, and celebrating a supper of oneness and unity? Surely the latter is the case. Then how could he have meant that only men might celebrate the supper and women would be excluded?

Third: Saint Paul said that women must keep silent in church. Then how could a woman preside at the reading of the word and at the Eucharist?

Three passages from Saint Paul come under consideration here.[21]

. . . Any woman who prays or prophesies with her head uncovered brings shame upon her head [1 Cor. 11:5].

According to the rule observed in all the assemblies of believers, women should keep silent in such gatherings. They may not speak. Rather, as the law states, submissiveness is indicated for them. If they want to learn anything, they should ask their husbands at home. It is a disgrace when a woman speaks in the assembly [1 Cor. 14:34–35].

A woman must listen in silence and be completely submissive. I do not permit a woman to act as teacher, or in any way to have authority over a man: she must be quiet [1 Tim. 2:11–12].

These passages seem clear enough. We can dispense with any discussion of women's access to the priesthood. Paul would seem to have resolved the matter. Women may not even teach. Surely they cannot consecrate.[22]

Taken out of context, this is what these assertions may suggest. But they must be interpreted within the world in which they were written, where women simply had no civil rights. This culture is in Saint Paul's blood and bones. He mirrors the situation of his time. It could not have been any other way. To seek to draw a timeless norm from these temporally determined assertions would be to freeze history, and thus to destroy it.

The Christian faith transcends all particular times. Yet it always appears within a particular time, and within the coordinates of understanding, customs, laws, and roles of that time and its various human groups. The faith sacralizes none of these incarnations. It enters them, but is not lost in them. We must always distinguish between faith and theology, between the Christian message and its social expression, between Christianity and its incarnation in a determined, limited linguistic and cultural universe. These distinctions have an indispensable value for the present discussion of the position of women in the church. They are absolutely necessary if we are to understand Christianity's basic intention, which is never the sacralization of particular cultural expressions.

Now let us move to an analysis of the texts. The first passage, 1 Corinthians 11:5, causes no difficulties. Here Paul guarantees women, contrary to Judaic tradition, the right to prophesy in the church community. But they are to exercise their right in conformity with the prevailing norms of decency and good taste. Today these norms would have no meaning, as the veil is no longer standard accouterment for worship.

Paul argues further in a fashion that to us today no longer has validity. "Does not nature itself teach you that it is dishonorable for a man to wear his hair long, while the long hair of a woman is her glory?" (1 Cor. 11:14). This statement, like others of Paul's in women's regard, is the product of a type of understanding that neither need be nor can be ours any longer, especially in a world in which, like ours, men, and even ecclesiastics, including Pope Pius X, wear their hair gloriously long, without this being considered an assault on human nature.

The second text, 1 Corinthians 14:34–35, has been subjected to two different exegeses. The first, which is gradually gaining ground, holds that these two verses referring to women are the interpolation of a Jewish Christian.[23] The argument advanced is worthy of consideration. The admonition interrupts the Pauline discourse, which treats of order in the community and, specifically, when one should speak and when keep silent. It is prophets who come in for this animadversion in a special way. If we omit the text referring to women, seeing that their situation has already been handled in 1 Corinthians 11, we find the first part of the discourse on speech and silence connecting much more logically with the second, thus:

> You can all speak your prophecies, but one by one, so that all may be instructed and encouraged. The spirits of the prophets are under the prophets' control, since God is a God, not of confusion, but of peace. [Here we omit verses 34–35, the passage concerning the silence of women.] Did the preaching of God's word originate with you? Are you the only ones to whom it has come? If anyone thinks he is a prophet or a man of the Spirit, he should know that what I have written you is the Lord's commandment [1 Cor. 14:31–33, 36–38].

Strikingly, we now have a strictly logical order of thought. Thus, textual order suggests that the two verses on women do indeed constitute an interpolation. To boot, "assembly of believers" in verse 34 is a technical expression dear to the Jewish Christian communities—in which, indeed, women would have been bound by the Mosaic law always to keep silent in cultural assemblies.

In light of all this, proponents of the first exegesis do not attribute the prohibition in question to Paul, especially since this would also attribute to the apostle a plain self-contradiction: in 1 Corinthians 11:5, as we have seen, he does allow women to speak in church.

The second exegesis, by contrast with the one we have just been considering, admits the Pauline authenticity of the whole of chapter 14. Paul is saved from contradicting himself in another way. This approach begins by noting that the whole of chapter 14 falls, as it were, under the rubric of order in the community, with the guiding principle that everything done in the community is to be done in such a way as to "edify"—that is, to be done "with a constructive purpose" (v. 26; cf. vv. 3, 4, 5, 12, 17). In this context, it is not only women who are commanded to "keep silent in such gatherings" (*en tais ekklēsiais si-*

gatōsan, v. 34), but anyone speaking in tongues, as well (*sigatō en ekklēsia*), unless someone is present to interpret (v. 28). When anyone in the community receives a revelation, it is this person who is to speak while the prophet keeps still (*sigatō*, v. 30). In this context of order and discipline, we are told by the exegetes who champion this second interpretation, women too are enjoined to keep silent (vv. 34–36)—when their speech would not be to a "constructive purpose" (v. 26). Can we think that Paul feels that women can never speak with a constructive purpose? Neither, therefore, say our exegetes, may we suppose that he wished to keep them from ever speaking in the community. In this interpretation, Paul would not be laying down any blanket prohibition forbidding women to speak. He would only be forbidding them to speak idly, exactly as with all the other prohibitions of the extended passage.

There remains the third text, 1 Timothy 2:11–12: "A woman must listen in silence. . . . I do not permit a woman to act as a teacher. . . . "

At first glance the words seem completely clear. However, they lend themselves to distortion at the hands of an ideological interpretation bent on justifying something that still goes on in our own day. If women today were permitted to speak out as they should be permitted (of course, today they may speak, but let us suppose that they could be even more outspoken than they can actually be), certainly this text would not be seen as an impediment to their so doing, nor would their speech be viewed as disobedience to a Pauline admonition!

Let us say simply: We must understand Paul, or his disciple, the author of this letter, within a context of generalized discrimination against women. For this is exactly what we find in the immediate context of the passage enjoining silence on women. After all, just above, the sacred writer has made this reproach: "The women should dress modestly and quietly, and not be decked out in fancy hair styles, gold ornaments, pearls, or costly clothing; rather, as becomes women who profess to be religious, their adornment should be good deeds" (1 Tim. 2:9–10). We tend to forget these two verses. They do not seem to apply to our day. What could be wrong with women's cosmetics and jewelry, as we see them around us? Surely divine revelation is not concerned to erect such considerations into eternal principles. But of course when it comes to women speaking up in our church—ah, that is a different matter altogether. This is divine law, we hear, forever and always.

Why is theology so concerned with women's silence, and it ignores their toilette? Is it not because 1 Timothy 2:11–12 lends itself to the ideological justification of a religious status to which males alone have access? Further: this same letter lays down that for the consecration of a bishop, a man must be selected who has been "married only once," and who can "keep his children under control without sacrificing his dignity" (1 Tim. 3:2, 4). Where do we have this in the church? Suppose, hypothetically, that somewhere in the Brazilian church a married man were to be ordained a bishop, with all the canonical rites and correct intention. The church would consider his consecration valid. But if a woman were to be so ordained, her ordination would be considered invalid, perhaps precisely in virtue of 1 Timothy 2:11–12. Why does the church not observe the very clear prescriptions concerning widows in 1 Timothy 5:3–16?

The answer is simple, and universally accepted. The church does not observe the precepts concerning widows because in our society widows do not have the same religious and social function as they did in apostolic times. What bishop today could repeat what we find in 1 Timothy 6:1? "All under the yoke of slavery," we read, "must regard their masters as worthy of full respect; otherwise the name of God and the church's teaching suffer abuse." The church would not cite this text in addressing modern oppressors, because it understands that this message, too, is conditioned by the world of the time in which it was composed, when slavery constituted an unquestionable social institution. Now, just as we interpret these passages about married bishops and widows and slaves within the hermeneutic universe of those times, so also our exegesis of the passage concerning the status of women in the church must respect that other universe. Otherwise we shall be fostering an ideology of ecclesial status. It is not a case of *jus divinum*, but simply of *jus ecclesiasticum*, and it is reformable.

Fourth: In church tradition, there have never been priestesses. Even Our Lady was not one.

It is true that tradition practically never speaks of priestesses. It does tell us of deaconesses, who were commissioned for the ministry, especially from the end of the fourth century on, through an ordination by imposition of hands, and who belonged to the hierarchy of the church. Their charge was not only women's baptism, with its pastoral preparation, but they were also permitted to read the Epistle and Gospel, wear the stole, and distribute communion. In the eleventh century their ordination rite was exactly parallel with that for the deacons.[24] There is reference to Christian priestesses among the Priscillians, but this is expressly combated by the Synod of Nimes, A.D. 394. Pope Gelasius, writing to the bishops of southern Italy in 494, condemns abuses on the part of certain women who "serve at holy altars" and perform "everything which is entrusted to the service of men."[25]

In this latter instance, we are no longer speaking of deaconesses, but of genuine priestly orders. However, this praxis was not accepted. Church tradition prolonged the situation women had had from the beginning. No further speculation was entertained in the matter, nor did women themselves remonstrate. Haye van der Meer, who has studied in detail the teaching of tradition in this material, says:

> Nowhere in the entire Patristic literature on the priesthood of woman did we meet any deliberation that rejected the priesthood of woman on *essential* grounds. We found only considerations such as these: apostles sent forth no women; Mary did not baptize Jesus; Eve was seduced; woman did once teach man—in paradise—and nothing but damnation came from that; Paul forbade it; and so on.[26]

"But Mary was not a priest." Mary did not receive the sacrament of order, nor would it have made any sense for her to receive it, since she possessed a priesthood superior to that of any sacramental priest. As Coredemptrix and Mediatrix, she has always been considered a priest, *eminentiori modo.*[27] Since Mary's priesthood was so much higher than that of the ministers of the church, the fact that she was not sacramentally ordained can scarcely be invoked as an argument for women's exclusion from the sacrament of order. For Mary, the fact of never having celebrated Mass was not a deprivation. She did much more than merely celebrate Mass. She was Mother of God, she carried and offered up her own Son, and together with him was constituted the principle of our salvation.

Conclusion: The permanence of the custom does not imply a doctrinal tradition.

From the reflections we have entertained, we may draw the following conclusions:

a. From the hermeneutical-exegetical point of view, there is no decisive scriptural argument to exclude women from priestly ordination.

b. Tradition contains no basic theological principle to justify the concentration of the priesthood today in the hands of men exclusively. It is sufficiently clear that the present state is due to a historico-sociological development within which, however, woman has gradually become aware of her equality with man and has thereby begun to transcend the barriers of discrimination that Christianity itself has endorsed. Woman's exclusion from the priesthood has reflected her inferior position in society.

c. Thus we are dealing not with doctrinal tradition, but with the permanence of a 2,000-year-old custom that is susceptible of alteration at the hands of a new consciousness of woman's dignity and of the collaboration she can furnish in the church. As Cardinal Daniélou concluded: "Nothing decisive was brought forward against women's priesthood. The study may proceed. . . ."[28]

d. Taking its point of departure in this new understanding of woman, the Lutheran Church has been ordaining women priests and ministers for a quarter of a century now. Likewise, with somewhat more hesitation it is true, the Episcopal Church has ordained women priests. In 1971, in Cincinnati, Ohio, Sally Jane Priesand was ordained a rabbi, and a tradition older than Christian tradition fell. In the Catholic Church, religious women in some places have taken on all of the priestly functions except the consecration of the Eucharist and the imparting of sacramental absolution.[29] This was a huge step. Where might this road lead?

Women's Priesthood: Not the Same as Men Exercise It Today

It is not enough to point to the possibility of women's ordination to the priesthood. To what sort of priesthood are women to be ordained? Today's concrete priesthood in the Catholic Church bears the brand of male celibacy, and that brand is deeply ingrained. R.J.A. van Eyden has written: "The

Church—or at least her hierarchy—is often called a solicitous mother. It is an image that looks a little empty when the motherly care is ultimately exercised only by men."[30]

All official faith institutions are male in their tone. It would be a sad mistake for women to seek to take on the concrete historical image of the priest as it has actually been lived by men. Here "women's variants" enter into play. Flowing from their specific difference, their whole charge of femininity, on the levels of the ontological, the psychological, the sociological, the biological, and so on, entail a demand for a historical concretization of women's priesthood as *women's* priesthood. Women neither can nor should simply replace male priests. They should articulate their priesthood in their own way.

The Brazilian experience, with religious women in charge of parishes, can be meaningful in two ways. First, it bears witness to a church that has opened up to the liberation of woman, grasps her Christian maturity, and so can entrust to her the care of a local church. Second, this experience establishes a critical grid through which to examine existing priestly institutions. Will they be adequate for women? Will they permit the religious woman to express the wealth of her femaleness, from which the church itself dare not prescind? Or shall we instead have a case of "poor grafting," to the detriment of all concerned, men, women, and the church? The Brazilian experience testifies to a veritable impasse.

The opinion of Elizabeth Gössmann, who specializes in this material, is of particular significance: "Let us be quite clear about the fact that a woman is simply not suited to ecclesiastical office as we know it today. Only when it has been transformed from within, and reconstituted in relation to the community as a whole, might it become something transferable to women."[31]

Theological Considerations Bearing on Women's Priesthood

The foregoing reflections point up the fact that when we speak of women's priesthood it is not simply a matter of claiming for women a place that has been denied them for many centuries. It is a matter of analyzing whether, in the movement of our world, where woman is gradually achieving more and more equality to men in dignity and rights, a priestly function is also appropriate for her.

Women discharge many functions in society and the church. Should the priesthood be included? Or does an immovable wall cut women off from that priesthood? Dogmatically, as we have seen, there is no obstacle. Discrimination against women in civil society is slowly but surely wearing away. Will the church, sociologically, in the organization of its power and the exercise of its pastoral charge, change—or will it remain the fortress of conservatism and a stagnant backwater of structures of a world definitively passé?

Today's world is coming to understand very well—thanks in large part to the influence of Christian ideals—that "the good of men and women are interdependent. Both suffer injury when, in any community, either cannot contribute to the full measure of his or her capacities."[32] The church itself would sustain a wound in its organic body if it refused to allow room in its institutions for the wealth of woman, with her maturity of faith. Even if there were enough priests, or if a mature adult lay ministry flourished in the church—one that would be capable, in the name of its own faith, to carry the cause of Christ forward in the midst of the world—even then the question of women and the priesthood would have to be raised. Without women there would be a flaw in the church. The church would be deprived of riches that woman alone can offer it.

We are in no way attempting to specify the function of women in the church. This would be to speak from outside the situation: indeed it would be oppression, since it would be an attempt to establish a predetermined functioning, within which woman would find her place. The path to be followed runs in precisely the opposite direction. No one can be expected to fit into a pre-established function in such a context. It is urgent that we open our eyes to the new self-understanding being developed by women, and to a global social process that tends less and less to privilege one sex over the other. We must be attentive, therefore, to the new function of the sexes, and not to the old function of men and women. We are creating a new society. If man's function is not modified, woman's will not be either—and vice versa. It is imperative to raise people's consciousness with regard to the proper, specific function of the sexes, with their differences. Then we shall have new functions, even in the church.

In this task, women are "on their own." No longer will anyone "tell them what to do." Today, all of us, men and women alike, are searching for our identity within a relentlessly accelerating process of social change. We must be patient enough not to concoct hasty, inadequate answers.

Theology's task is not primarily to chart courses, but to let courses chart themselves as they are carried forward in the hushed love of God and reveal the meaning of their own direction. Theology will accept human consciousness-raising as a challenge, an opportunity for new incarnations of the Christian message. Christianity does not choose its world. But any world, and the whole world, is an opportunity for Christianity's historicization.

The changes in question are not taking place only in culture or only with regard to women, but in the church, as well, and with regard to its ministries. Without a doubt, a new understanding of the services and *diakonias* in the church will broaden the horizon of ministry itself, in such a way as also to reveal the value of its exercise by women for the good of the whole church community.

Universal Priesthood of Women

There is a theology of priesthood that is not very different from ideology. It reflects on only one type of priesthood—the form of priesthood that currently exists in the church—and yet makes it the only possible priesthood. This theology does not ask whether, in the light of the *ipsissima intentio Jesu*, in the light of Christian positivity and faith, the church, faced as it is with new cultural situations, could or could not permit other styles and even other understandings of the priestly mission. Vatican Council II laid a solid foundation, with serious structural consequences, for the "revaluation" of the concept of the church as People of God, and the universal priesthood of the faithful. By placing the chapter on the church as People of God first, ahead of the chapter on the hierarchical church, the council sought to teach that all power in the church is to be understood and exercised only from within, and in the service of, God's People. By proclaiming the universal priesthood of the faithful, the council raised a theological question that to this day has not found an adequate response: namely, What is the relationship between the universal priesthood and the ministerial priesthood?

In order to come to a more adequate grasp of the dimensions of priesthood, we must approach it along a more open horizon than that against which it is ordinarily seen.[33] Then it will appear as an opportunity for women as well.

A priest is a mediator and reconciler of divergent realities. Priests have a feeling of existing and living in an atmosphere of basic estrangement: they have to face God and face others, face surrounding reality and face themselves. The drama of human life is shot through with division and lies; life longs for oneness, for peace and concord between the universe and its profound meaning. The priest seeks to be the crucible of the common experience of all human beings, seeks to live from this experience and for its successful outcome. Therefore the priest lives apart from the world, not out of contempt for the world but in order to fulfill a mission of oneness and mediation for the world.

Jesus Christ, who was a layperson (cf. Heb. 7:13–14), took upon himself this task of reconciliation. He lived an existence so profound, so deep, that it reconciled human beings with God. He preached of love, renunciation of the spirit of revenge and hatred, and universal reconciliation, even with one's enemies (Mt. 5:45). He was a person-for-others to the end (Jn. 13:1). The novelty of his *diakonia* of reconciliation resides in the fact of its not having had to operate in the sphere of worship alone, but of having operated in the global sphere of life—in daily life with the masses, in preaching to them, in meeting and confrontation with persons, in prayer, in life, in death. Jesus' death on the cross, the consequence of his loyalty to God's cause, which was love and forgiveness, is our best example of gift of self and sacrifice for others, even for enemies. With his resurrection, Jesus continues his reconciling presence with human beings forever more.

The primitive community understood this well. In Jesus, God has reconciled all things (Col. 1:20), has unified the world, razing all barriers (Eph. 2:14). He has actualized that which had been the hope of all priesthood: definitive reconciliation of the human being with God and with other human beings. And he has done so to perfection (Heb. 9:26; 1 Pet. 3:18). In virtue of this his saving action, he who was sociologically a layperson is become the "great priest" (Heb. 10:21) and the "one mediator" (1 Tim. 2:5).[34]

Priesthood, then, is not a state, but a mode of existence. It is an existence that reconciles. Because Jesus, by his life, death, and resurrection, lived, exhaustively and eschatologically, the dimension of reconciliation, oneness, and love, he is called "high priest" forever (Heb. 6:20).

A Christian is a person seeking to lead a life in conformity with the life of Jesus Christ, and with the vitality that was manifested in that life. Therefore every Christian life is a priestly life. By faith and the sacraments we are rendered sharers in the priesthood of Christ.[35] And not only of his life: we become sharers in all the richness of his *diakonia*, his proclamation, and his deed of sanctification.[36] In other words, the Christian is responsible for the mission of the whole church. He or she is responsible for proclamation by word and example: for making the world holy, for enhancing and fostering the order and harmony of the community.

In the church, before any differentiation comes fundamental equality. All are in Christ, all form his holy people, all share in his priesthood of reconciliation. If by "lay" we understand, as the Greek word reminds us, the "people" (*laos*) of God, then all in the church are basically "lay people": popes, bishops, priests, and simple faithful. All are members of God's people. Accordingly, the difference between hierarchy and laity is not primary but secondary. It can obtain only within a basic equality and at the service of and for the purpose of equality—not over the people and independently of the people.

The universal priesthood of the faithful is not a phenomenon of the cultic level alone. To be sure, in worship this priesthood finds its most exalted expression, but it must be lived on the vaster horizon of life as well, as Jesus Christ lived it. It was not only his death on the cross that was redemptive. His whole existence, in the cultic and profane alike, in his preaching and in his everyday life, was reconciling, hence priestly. This is why Saint Paul could admonish the Romans: " . . . Offer your bodies as a living sacrifice holy and acceptable to God" (Rom. 12:1).

In the concrete case of Christian women, everything can take on a function of priesthood and reconciliation. For instance, their care for their children, their *diakonia* in the upbuilding of family harmony, and of course their professional life, which brings them in contact with other persons; teacher, nurse, physician, secretary, salesperson—whatever the profession—can be priestly in this sense. For a Christian a profession is more than just a way of earning one's daily bread. It is a way of actualizing service, concord, and reconciliation among human beings. It is a means of bringing human beings nearer one another, in the transcendence of divisions, and in humble, hushed acceptance of anguishing and inescapable situations.

The *diakonia* of reconciliation is to be exercised by all Christians. This makes them priests, men as well as women, for they are all to prolong in time and space the unifying function of Christ, the eternal High Priest.

Ministerial Priesthood, the Principle of Unity in the Community

The type of priesthood we have been considering can cause women no difficulties. The problem arises when the question of the ministerial priesthood is broached, that is, the priesthood proper to men ordained by the sacrament of order. What is the specificity that distinguishes these men from the other members of God's priestly people? Can women have access to their priest-hood?

There is a classic understanding of ministerial priesthood, still maintained by the document of the Bishops' Synod on the Ministerial Priesthood (1971), which defines the essential status of priest merely in itself, without any immedi-ate reference to the People of God.[37] By priestly ordination the priest is rendered the official representative of Christ.

> . . . Through the ministry of the bishop, God consecrates priests so that they can share by a special title in the priesthood of Christ. Thus, in performing sacred functions they can act as the ministers of [Christ] . . . .[38]

The priest is specified by his *power* to consecrate. The horizon against which this power is perceived resides in the cultic and sacramental sphere. This is tantamount to a reduction of the rich meaning of the priesthood of Jesus Christ, which is not restricted to worship alone. It must be lived in the complete context of life, for it is to be, whole and entire, a priesthood of oneness, peace, and reconciliation.

Correctly analyzed, ordination does not properly confer a power for wor-ship and consecration. It is not the priest who consecrates, baptizes, or for-gives. It is Christ who forgives, baptizes, and consecrates. Priests lend their persons and their faculties in order that the invisible Christ may become sacramentally visible. The ministerial priesthood is not a power to consecrate; it is the power officially to represent the one, eternal priesthood of Jesus Christ. The sacrament of order raises a particular person to the dignity of this function.

What relationship, then, obtains between the ministerial priesthood and the priestly People of God? We must not conceptualize the former as something outside of, above, or independent of the People of God. Its function is not determined by its sacramental powers in contrast to people deprived of these powers. The point of departure must be ecclesiological and communitarian. It is as a service to the church that the ministerial priesthood exists, not as something independent of it.

The church community arises as the universal sacrament of salvation. Through all its institutions, through word, through sacraments, it is to render present the reconciliation brought by Jesus Christ. All the faithful are cores-ponsible for this mission, not only the ordained. In this community in Christ, differences of nation, intelligence, and sex are of no consideration whatever (Gal. 3:28). All are "sent," without distinction. Equality prevails here, and a basic brotherly and sisterly communion of all, in Christ and because of Christ. This basic equality does not mean that everyone does everything. The church is an organized community of equals, in which tasks are hierarchical.

There is a diversity of charisms in the church. Charisms, for Paul, are synonymous with functions. " . . . Each one has his own gift (*charisma*) from God, one this and another that" (1 Cor. 7:7). But each such "manifestation of the Spirit is given for the common good" (1 Cor. 12:7). These charisms, or functions, pertain to the essential structure of the church in such wise that a church without charisms is not the church of Christ. But there is a simultaneity of charisms in the church, and here the question arises: To whom does it fall to watch over the unity of the charisms? The charism of unity ought to be at the service of all the charisms, that all things may concur for order, harmony, and the common utility. The New Testment speaks of the charism of direction and governance (1 Cor. 12:28), and of those who preside in the community (1 Thess. 5:12; Rom. 12:8; 1 Tim. 5:17). The presbyters (the elders), the bishops, (*episkopoi*), and the deacons are the vehicles, or vessels, of the charism of unity, of oneness, in the community.

In this charism the specificity of the presbyter/priest resides. Theirs is the charism of coordinating the various functions—the various charisms—within the community, ordering them all to the good of the church. This they do by furthering some, encouraging others, and discovering charisms already present of which the community is not yet conscious. They may warn certain persons that they are placing the community at peril. Priests do not accumulate all functions for themselves. They integrate all services in a single unity.[39]

The presbyterate, therefore, is the principal vehicle of responsibility for the unity of the local church, be this unity expressed in the *diakonia* of concrete love through aid to sisters and brothers in need, in the context of community services, in the service of proclamation by catechesis, homiletics, and enrichment courses, or in the service of worship and sacrament. In all things priests should be solicitous for oneness and harmony, so that the community may be one body in Christ Jesus (Rom. 12:5).

In terms of this interpretation, what specifies the ministerial priesthood is not the faculty or act of consecrating, not the authority or act of teaching, but the task and actuality of constituting the community's oneness in its worship and in its proclamation of the Good News. By reason of this charism of theirs, however, it belongs to priests to exercise the presidency at the celebration and authority in preaching.

The function of the priest in the local church is the same as the function of the bishop in the regional church and the pope in the universal church. Each is constituted *principium unitatis visibile*. Is it permissible that this function of procuring unity be exercised exclusively by men? Modern history and sheer fact have shown us that women easily have the same capabilities as men, not only in civil government, but in the experiments, already under way in the church, of religious women who have assumed the direction of a local church. Women discharge the role of procurer of unity in their own female way— differently from men, but achieving the same reality: harmony, good functioning, and unity in the community of believers.

Promotion to the sacrament of order raises a given person in the community to the assignment of presiding, in oneness and reconciliation, at the various services. All should be solicitous for this oneness. But the priest, male or female, is officially thrust forward, set before the community, in order to be head, in the name of Jesus Christ himself, of the *diakonia* of reconciliation and unification in the community. The sacrament confers nothing exclusive, nothing that can be attained only through this sacrament, so that without this sacrament the church simply could not have this grace. It confers a more profound visibility upon a reality that must be sought by all in the community: oneness and love. Therefore, in the sacrament of order, as in the other sacraments, a strict relationship between the function of all the faithful and the function of the priest prevails.

It belongs to priests to preside at the assembly, in worship and in the eucharistic celebration. It falls to them officially to represent Christ the Head, the Source of unity. It likewise falls to them, par excellence, to consecrate and celebrate the Most Holy Eucharist.

If a woman can be the principle of unity, as she is in so many communities, then theologically there is nothing to stand in the way of her empowerment, through ordination, to consecrate, to render Christ sacramentally present at the heart of the community's worship.[40] The manner in which she will do so calls for no description here. No apostolic theory will be able to make such a description. Only concrete experience, and life in a determinate context, will show the precise manner in which she will acquit herself of her task.

The Human Being, including the Religious Human Being: Animus and Anima

The view we have been developing postulates the priest, male and female, at the heart of the human and ecclesial community. The communitarian essence of priesthood is attested to by the oldest New Testament tradition. Even the Council of Chalcedon (A.D. 451), in its Sixth Canon, stated expressly:

No one shall be ordained at large, either to the presbyterate, or diaconate, or to any place in the ecclesiastical order whatsoever; nor unless the person ordained be particularly designated to some church in a city, or village, or to some martyr's chapel, or monastery. And if any have been ordained without charge, the holy Synod has decreed such ordination to be null and nowhere operative, to the reproach of the ordainer.[41]

What we have attempted to do in this book is to show that there are no decisive arguments against women's access to the ministerial priesthood. This negative finding is reinforced by our thesis that an adequate understanding of this ministerial priesthood, in the light of the priesthood of Christ, does not posit its specificity in the power to consecrate, but in being the principle of unity in the community. A woman can exercise this *diakonia* as well as a man.

Woman's position in the church should keep pace with the evolution of her position in civil society. That society tends more and more to accord women an equality with men. Any discrimination on grounds of biological or cultural differentiation becomes more and more unseemly and intolerable. The church, which rightly calls itself *catholica*, simply may not, in virtue of its very catholicity, maintain its traditional prohibitions here.

An enriched reflection on the *munus*, the task and charge of representing salvation in Jesus Christ, ought to encourage male ecclesiastics to have the humility to recognize that Christ's "fullness of divinity and humanity" cannot be exhausted in its masculine representation. Modern anthropology has served notice, backed by sound reasoning, that we can no longer naïvely speak of exclusively "masculine" and "feminine" qualities. The human being is always masculine and feminine, in intimate reciprocal relation, varying in their mutual proportion in each individual human existence. A right human personalization and maturation demand and suppose that a man gradually grow to a better expression of his anima—the feminine element in the male—and a woman to that of her animus, her masculine element. Thus it will be to men's own fulfillment to create more space for women's freedom and liberation. As for woman, her capacity to represent the male Jesus Christ is guaranteed by the fact that he, like the rest of humankind—including all males—possessed in his humanity dimensions of both the male and the female. Only thus will the prophetic words of Saint Paul be verified in our living history: "There does not exist among you . . . male or female. All are one in Christ Jesus" (Gal. 3:28).

Addendum

Under date of October 15, 1976, the Sacred Congregation for the Doctrine of the Faith published a "Declaration on the Question of the Admission of Women to the Ministerial Priesthood." This document reaffirms traditional doctrine, as against the strong tendency of theological investigation to favor the admission of women to the priestly ministry. The document issues from an official, authoritative source. It enjoys a special authority—higher than that of any theologian. But according to the criteria of the dogmatic value of official documents, it is not infallible. Therefore it can contain error, as the history of less-than-infallible documents shows. In admitting this, we shall be neither adding to nor subtracting from the authority of this document. With all respect, theology may—indeed, it is its task to do so—study the weight of the argumentation presented. This is what Karl Rahner does with such aplomb in his critical comments on this declaration of the Sacred Congregation.[42] Rahner concludes that the arguments adduced are not theologically convincing, hence do not settle the matter. The question remains open, and discussion may continue.[43] The declaration's basic argument against women's access to the ministerial priesthood is that neither Christ nor the apostles included women in the apostolic college. The document denies that this circumstance belongs to the sociohistorical conditioning of the age, and therefore translates the will of Jesus. The tradition of faith is read as bearing out the current praxis of the church.

It is precisely this last point that must be proved, not presupposed. The declaration leaves the burden of proof to those who allege such conditionings, instead of assuming this burden itself, which would have been the proper way to proceed. Furthermore, the concept of priesthood is practically restricted to its cultural-liturgical aspect, whereas theology, even at official levels—as we have shown—considers priesthood in a broader perspective of service to the unity of the church at all levels. The document constitutes a step in the discussion; it does not close the matter. It may have succeeded in postponing a solution, but theology, while according the declaration the most serious consideration and holding it in the highest esteem, may continue to develop its reasons both pro and contra.

Notes

1. A New Experience of Church

1. Yves M. -J. Congar, "Os grupos informais na Igreja," in Alfonso Gregory, ed., *Comunidades eclesiais de base: utopia ou realidade?* (Petrópolis, Brazil: Vozes, 1973), pp. 144–45.
2. Pedro Demo, *Relatório da pesquisa sobre as comunidades eclesiais de base,* pp. 18–19.
3. Pope Paul VI, in statement appearing in *Revista Eclesiástica Brasileira* 34 (1974): 945.
4. Congar, "Grupos informais," pp. 129–30.
5. Cf. José Marins, "Comunidades eclesiais de base na América Latina," in Concilium 104 (Portuguese edition, 1975), pp. 22–25.
6. Brazilian Bishops Conference, *Plano pastoral de conjunto (1962-1965),* p. 58.
7. See the whole issue of Concilium 104 (Portuguese edition, 1975). Cf. the apostolic exhortation, *Evangelii Nuntiandi,* no. 58 (Pope Paul VI, *On Evangelization in the Modern World* [Washington, D.C.: United States Catholic Conference, 1976], pp. 40–42). Cf. also the declaration of the Synod of Bishops in 1974, *Evangelization in the Modern World,* no. 12 (in Joseph Gremillion, ed., *The Gospel of Peace and Justice: Catholic Social Teaching since Pope John* [Maryknoll, N.Y.: Orbis Books, 1976], pp. 597–98).
8. Marins, "Comunidades eclesiais," p. 27.
9. Demo, article in *Comunidades. Igreja na base,* Estudos da CNBB no. 3 (São Paulo: Paulinas, 1975), pp. 67–110.
10. Ibid., p. 110.
11. Ibid., p. 79.
12. Ibid., p. 93.
13. Ibid., p. 92.

2. Church, or Merely Ecclesial Elements?

1. Alfonso Gregory, "Dados preliminares sobre experiências de CEB's no Brasil," in Alfonso Gregory, ed., *Comunidades eclesiais de base: utopia ou realidade?* (Petrópolis, Brazil: Vozes, 1973), pp. 47–100, esp. pp. 53 ff.
2. José Marins, "Comunidades eclesiais de base na América Latina," in Concilium 104 (Portuguese edition, 1975), p. 20.
3. Marins, "Comunidad eclesial de base," mimeographed (Lima, 1972), p. 318. By the same author: *Iglesia local: comunidad de base* (Buenos Aires: Bonum, 1969).
4. Alberto Antoniazzi, "Reflexões teológicas sobre as comunidades eclesiais de base," in *Comunidades: Igreja na base,* Estudos da CNBB no. 3 (São Paulo: Paulinas, 1975), p. 130.

5. Louis Billot, *De Ecclesia Christi* (Rome, 1927), p. 451. Cf. Charles Journet, vol. 2 of *The Church of the Word Incarnate: An Essay in Speculative Theology*, trans. A. H. C. Downes (London and New York: Sheed and Ward, 1955). Cf. also Yves M.-J. Congar's critique in *Mysterium Salutis*, vol. 4/3 (Petrópolis, Brazil: Vozes, 1972), p. 41, n. 83.

6. *Christus Dominus*, no. 11 (in Walter M. Abbott, ed., *The Documents of Vatican II* [New York: Herder and Herder, 1966], p. 403).

7. *Lumen Gentium*, no. 26 (in Abbott, *Documents II*, p. 50).

8. Cf. B. Neunheuser, "Igreja universal e Igreja local," in G. Baraúna, ed., *A Igreja do Vaticano II* (Petrópolis: Vozes, 1965), pp. 650–74; E. Lanne, "L'Eglise locale et l'Eglise universelle," *Irénikon*, 1970, pp. 481ff.

9. Medellín document on "Joint Pastoral Planning," in vol. 2 of Louis Michael Colonnese, ed., *The Church in the Present-Day Transformation of Latin America in the Light of the Council* (Washington, D.C.: United States Catholic Conference, 1968–69), 15:10–11.

10. Ibid., 15:10.

11. "La notion d'Eglise particulière," in *Synodus Episcoporum—Comitato per l'Informazione,* communiqués 11, 16 (Rome, October 1974); or in *Documentation Catholique,* no. 1667 (January 1975).

12. In Baggio's "De accuratiore usu verbi Ecclesiae 'particularis' et 'localis,' " manuscript (Rome, 1974).

13. Cf. *Ad Gentes*, no. 22 (in Abbott, *Documents*, p. 612).

14. *Lumen Gentium*, no. 26 (Abbott, *Documents*, p. 50).

15. Henri de Lubac, *Las Iglesias particulares en la Iglesia universal* (Salamanca, 1974), pp. 45–48. French original: *Les églises particulières dans l'Eglise universelle* (Paris: Aubier Montaigne, 1971).

16. De Lubac, *Iglesias particulares*, pp. 31–43.

17. Saint Cyprian, *Letter* 65, chap. 4.

18. J. B. Libânio, *Igreja particular* (São Paulo: Loyola, 1974), p. 37.

19. Henrique Vaz, *Fundamentos filosófico-histórico-antropológicos da noção de Igreja particular*, p. 168.

20. Cf. Hans Küng, *The Church*, trans. Ray and Rosaleen Ockenden (London: Burns & Oates, 1967), pp. 302–3.

21. Louis Bouyer, *The Church of God*, trans. Charles Underhill Quinn (Chicago: Franciscan Herald Press, 1982), p. 396.

22. Cf. the entire second part of H.-M. Legrand, "Le ministère èpiscopal: au service de l'Eglise locale et au service de l'Eglise universelle," in *Documents-Episcopat*, no. 1 (January 1975). The use of "portion" (Port., *porção*) instead of "part" comes from *Christus Dominus,* no. 11; for *portio* instead of *pars,* cf. also Abbott, *Documents,* p. 612.

23. Yves M.-J. Congar, "Os grupos informais na Igreja," in Gregory, *Comunidades eclesiais*, p. 142.

24. Cf. Karl Rahner, "The Concept of Mystery in Catholic Theology: First Lecture," in his *Theological Investigations*, vol. 4, trans. Kevin Smyth (London: Darton, Longman & Todd; New York: Seabury Press, 1974), pp. 46–48.

25. Cf. Gregory, "Dados preliminares," appendix 2, p. 85.

26. *Lumen Gentium*, no. 8 (in Abbott, *Documents,* p. 22).

27. Ibid., no. 2, p. 16.

28. Ibid., no. 16, p. 35.

29. Ibid.

30. Ibid.

31. Ibid., no. 15, pp. 33–34.

32. Ibid., no. 14, p. 33.

33. Cf. ibid., no. 8, p. 22; no. 14, p. 32.

34. Ibid., no. 1, p. 15; *Sacrosanctum Concilium,* no. 26 (in Abbott, *Documents,* p. 147).

35. *Lumen Gentium,* no. 8 (in Abbott, *Documents,* p. 22).

36. For this whole series of problems, see Leonardo Boff, *Die Kirche als Sakrament im Horizont der Welterfahrung: Versuch einer Legitimation und einer struktur-funktionalistischen Grundlegund der Kirche in Anschluss an das II. Vatikanische Konzil* (Paderborn: Bonifacius, 1972), pp. 275–95, 399–413.

37. Cf. the various expressions of communion between churches developed by tradition, as *litterae communicatoriae, fermentum,* or concelebration for the ordination of a bishop (see Congar, in *Mysterium Salutis,* pp. 45–49).

38. Cf. *Ad Gentes,* no. 4 (in Abbott, *Documents,* p. 588).

3. The Reinvention of the Church

1. Cf. Leonard Boff, "A Igreja, sacramento do Espírito Santo," in *O Espírito Santo* (Petrópolis, Brazil: Vozes, 1973).

2. "De Ecclesia particulari eiusque fidei testimonio," manuscript (Rome, October 1974). See the résumé of this document in *Prospective* (Brussels), 1975, no. 504.

3. *Ad Gentes,* no. 21 (in Walter M. Abbott, ed., *The Documents of Vatican II* [New York: Herder and Herder, 1966]. p. 610).

4. *Lumen Gentium,* no. 13 (in Abbott, *Documents,* pp. 31–32).

5. Hans Küng, "The Charismatic Structure of the Church," in *The Church and Ecumenism,* Concilium, vol. 4 (New York: Paulist Press, 1965), p. 59.

6. Gotthold Hasenhüttl, *Charisma, Ordnungsprinzip der Kirche* (Freiburg: Herder, 1969), p. 238.

7. See the Sixth Canon of the Council of Chalcedon, which may be found in *Translations and Reprints from the Original Sources of European History* (1900; reprint, Philadelphia: University of Pennsylvania, Department of History, n.d.), vol. 4, no. 2, p. 24.

8. Yves M.-J. Congar, *Ministères et communion ecclésiale* (Paris: Cerf, 1971), p. 19. Cf. A. Antoniazzi, *Os ministérios na Igreja hoje,* Cadernos de Teologia Pastoral no. 1 (Petrópolis, Brazil: Vozes, 1975), pp. 11–24.

9. Cf. Leonardo Boff, "As eclesiologias presentes nas CEBs," in various authors, *Uma Igreja que nasce do povo: comunidades eclesiais de base* (Petrópolis, Brazil: Vozes, 1975), pp. 201–9.

10. Cf. Carlos Alberto de Medina and Pedro A. Ribeiro de Oliveira, *Autoridade e participação: estudo sociológico da Igreja Católica* (Petrópolis, Brazil: CERIS/Vozes, 1973).

11. *Lumen Gentium,* no. 28 (in Abbott, *Documents,* p. 54).

12. Cf. de Medina and Ribeiro, *Autoridade e participação.* Cf. also de Medina, "A Igreja Católica no Brasil: uma perspectiva sociológica," *Revista Eclesiástica Brasileira,* 1973, pp. 72–91.

13. Cf. de Medina and Ribeiro, *Autoridade e participação,* pp. 59–132.

14. Ibid., 180–81.

15. *Ad Gentes*, no. 21 (in Abbott, *Documents*, p. 610).

16. José Comblin, "Processo de evolução para uma comunidade cristã urbana," in Alfonso Gregory, ed., *Comunidades eclesiais de base: utopia ou realidade?* (Petrópolis, Brazil: Vozes, 1973), p. 174. The same article appears in *Revista Eclesiástica Brasileira* 30 (1970): 819-28.

4. An Oppressed People Organizing for Liberation

1. Dietrich Bonhoeffer, *Letters and Papers from Prison,* enlarged edition, ed. Eberhard Bethge (New York: Macmillan, 1971), p. 300.

2. José Honório Rodrigues, *Concilião e reforma no Brasil* (São Paulo: Nacional, 1972).

3. Bonhoeffer, *Letters and Papers*, p. 300.

5. *Quaestio Disputata* I

1. C. Mesters, "O futuro de nosso passado," in various authors, *Uma Igreja que nasce do povo: comunidades eclesiais de base* (Petrópolis, Brazil: Vozes, 1975), p. 146.

2. Cf. Hans Conzelmann, *The Theology of St. Luke,* trans. Geoffrey Buswell (London: Faber and Faber, 1960).

3. Alfred Loisy, *The Gospel and the Church* (Philadelphia: Fortress Press, 1976).

4. Rudolf Schnackenburg, *God's Rule and Kingdom,* trans. John Murray (Freiburg: Herder, 1963); *The Church in the New Testament*, trans. W. J. O'Hara (New York: Herder and Herder, 1965).

5. Schnackenburg, *Church in the New Testament,* p. 188.

6. Cf. Patrick V. Dias, *Vielfalt der Kirche in der Vielfalt der Jünger, Zeugen und Diener* (Freiburg: 1968), p. 85. Our principal bibliography for the question of the historical Jesus and the church consists of: Schnackenburg, "Kirche," in *Lexikon für Theologie und Kirche,* 6:167-88; Anton Vögtle, "Jesus und die Kirche," in *Begegnung der Christen: Festschrift Otto Karrer* (Stuttgart/Freiburg, 1960), pp. 54-81; Otto Kuss, "Jesus und die Kirche im Neuen Testament," in *Auslegung und Verkündigung,* vol. 1 (Regensburg, 1963), pp. 25-77; J. Betz, "Die Gründung der Kirche durch den historischen Jesus," *Theologische Quartalschrift* 138 (1958): 152-83; Joseph Ratzinger, "O destino de Jesus e a Igreja," in *A Igreja em nossos dias* (São Paulo: Paulinas, 1969), pp. 9-29; J. Blank, "Die historische Jesus und die Kirche," *Wort und Wahrheit* 26 (1971): 291-307; Hans Küng, *The Church* (London: Burns & Oates, 1967), pp. 41-104; K. Müller, "Jesus von Nazareth und die Anfänge der Kirche," in various authors, *Die Aktion Jesu und die Re-Aktion der Kirche* (Wurzburg, 1972); J. Nolte, "Die Sache Jesu und die Zukunft der Kirche," in Franz Joseph Schierse, ed., *Jesus von Nazareth* (Mainz: Matthias-Grünewald, 1972), pp. 214-33.

7. Schnackenburg, "Kirche," 6:167.

8. Vögtle, "Jesus und die Kirche," pp. 57-58.

9. Küng, *The Church*, pp. 72, 74. Cf. Nolte, "Die Sache Jesu."

10. Rudolf Bultmann, *Theology of the New Testament,* trans. Kendrick Grobel, vol. 1 (London: SCM Press, 1952), p. 4.

11. Blank, "Der historische Jesus," p. 299. Cf. Müller, "Jesu Naherwartung und die Anfänge der Kirche," in various authors, *Aktion Jesu,* pp. 9-30.

12. Cf. Béda Rigaux, "Die Zwölf in Geschichte und Kerygma," in *Der historische Jesus und der kerygmatische Christus* (Berlin: Ristow-Matthiae, 1961), pp. 468-86;

Dias, *Vielfalt der Kirche*, pp. 174-99; H. Merklein, "Der Jünger-kreis Jesu," in various authors, *Aktion Jesu*, pp. 65-100.

13. Blank, "Der historische Jesus," p. 302.

14. Ratzinger, "Destino de Jesus." p. 14; Merklein, "Die eschatologisch-messianische Motivation der Jesusnachfolge," in various authors, in *Aktion Jesu*, pp. 87-89.

15. See Rudolf Pesch, "The Position and Significance of Peter in the Church of the New Testament," in *Papal Ministry in the Church,* ed. Hans Küng, Concilium vol. 64 (New York: Herder and Herder, 1971), pp. 21-35; Blank, "Der historische Jesus"; Dias, *Vielfalt der Kirche*. Cf. also H. Geist, "Jesus von Israel—der Ruf zur Sammlung," in various authors, *Aktion Jesu,* pp. 31-64.

16. Dias, *Vielfalt der Kirche,* p. 189.

17. Blank, "Der historische Jesus," p. 304.

18. Cf. Günther Bornkamm, "Die Binde- und Lösegewalt in der Kirche des Matthäus," in *Die Zeit der Kirche* (Freiburg, 1970), pp. 93-108.

19. Blank, "Der historische Jesus," p. 304; Pesch, "The Position and Significance of Peter," p. 30; Dias, *Vielfalt der Kirche,* pp. 188 ff.

20. Cf. Heinz Schuermann, *Der Abendmahlsbericht Lukas 22:7-38 als Gottesdienstordnung, Gemeindeordnung, Lebensordnung* (Paderborn: Schoeningh, 1957).

21. Rudolf Otto, *The Kingdom of God and the Son of Man,* trans. Floyd V. Filson and Bertram Lee-Woolf, rev. ed. (Boston: Starr King, 1957), pp. 265-66, 289.

22. Cf. Wolfgang Trilling, "Qué enseñó Jesús acerca del fin del mundo?", in *Jesús y los problemas de su historicidad* (Barcelona, 1970), pp. 126-47 (original: *Fragen zur Geschichtlichkeit Jesu,* 2nd ed. [Dusseldorf: Patmos, 1967]); O. Knoch, "Die eschatologische Frage, ihre Entwicklung und ihr gegenwärtiger Stand," *Biblische Zeitschrift* 6 (1962): 112-20; Norman Perrin, *Rediscovering the Teaching of Jesus* (New York: Harper & Row, 1967), pp. 154-206; Müller, "Jesu Naherwartung," pp. 9-30, esp. pp. 25-30.

23. Leonardo Boff, "O futuro do mundo: total cristificação e divinização," *Vozes,* 1972, pp. 565-67.

24. Erik Peterson, "Die Kirche aus Juden und Heiden," in *Theologische Traktate* (Munich: Kösel, 1957), pp. 411-29; Romano Guardini, *The Lord,* trans. Elinor Castendyk Briefs (Chicago: Regnery, 1954); and the following by Ratzinger: "Kirche," pp. 173-83; "Zeichen under den Völkern," in Michael Schmaus and Alfred Läpple, eds., *Wahrheit und Zeugnis* (Dusseldorf, 1964), pp. 456-66; *Introduction to Christianity,* trans. J. R. Foster (London: Burns & Oates, 1969); "Destino de Jesus"; *Das neue Volk Gottes: Entwürfe zur Ekklesiologie* (Dusseldorf, 1969), pp. 75-89.

25. Peterson, "Die Kirche," p. 411. See the similar opinion of Heinrich Schlier, "L'Option en faveur de la mission aux païens dans la chrétienté primitive," in *Le Temps de l'Eglise: Recherches d'exégèse* (Paris: Casterman, 1961), pp. 100-115 (original: *Die Zeit der Kirche: Exegetische Aufsätze und Vorträge* [Basel: Herder, 1966]).

26. Ratzinger, "Destino de Jesus," pp. 23-27.

27. Peterson, "Die Kirche," p. 412.

28. G. Lohfink, "Christologie und Geschichtsbild in Apg. 3, 19-21," *Biblische Zeitschrift* 13 (1969): 223-41.

29. Peterson, "Die Kirche," p. 417.

30. Ibid.

31. Küng, *The Church*, p. 76.

32. Leonardo Boff, "A Igreja Sacramento no Espírito Santo," *Grande Sinal* 26 (1972): 323-36.

33. Cf. Peterson, "Die Kirche," pp. 239–92.

34. Pope Paul VI, Closing Address to the 1974 Synod of Bishops, in *Revista Eclesiástica Brasileira* 34 (1974) 945.

6. *Quaestio Disputata* II

1. René Laurentin, *Nouveaux ministères et fin du clergé* (Paris, 1971), pp. 90–93.

2. Puebla Final Document, no. 629, in John Eagleson and Philip Scharper, eds., *Puebla and Beyond: Documentation and Commentary,* trans. John Drury (Maryknoll, N.Y.: Orbis Books, 1979), p. 211, citing *Evangelii Nuntiandi,* no. 58.

3. *Presbyterorum Ordinis,* no. 6 (in Walter M. Abbott, ed., *The Documents of Vatican II* [New York: Herder and Herder, 1966], p. 545).

4. *Unitatis Redintegratio,* no. 2 (in Abbott, *Documents,* p. 343).

5. *Lumen Gentium,* no. 3 (in Abbott, *Documents,* p. 16).

6. *Christus Dominus,* no. 30 (in Abbott, *Documents,* p. 418).

7. Christian life: *Lumen Gentium,* no. 11 (in Abbott, *Documents,* pp. 27–29); Evangelization: *Presbyterorum Ordinis,* no. 5 (in ibid., p. 542).

8. Cf. C. Mesters, "O futuro do nosso passado," in various authors, *Uma Igreja que nasce do povo: comunidades eclesiais de base* (Petrópolis, Brazil: Vozes, 1975), pp. 137ff.; P. A. Ribeiro de Oliveira, *O reconhecimento de novos ministérios* (Rio de Janeiro: CERIS, 1977), pp. 1–7.

9. Cf. H.-M. Legrand, "L'avenir des ministères: bilan, défis, tâches," *Le Supplement* 124 (1978): 21–48.

10. Henricus Denzinger, ed., *Enchiridion Symbolorum, Definitionum et Declarationum de Rebus Fidei et Morum,* 36th ed., rev. (Barcelona: Herder, 1976), nos. 794 (p. 256), 802 (p. 260), 1084 (p. 307).

11. Cf. G. H. Tavard, "The Function of the Minister in the Eucharistic Celebration," *Journal of Ecumenical Studies* 4 (1967): 629–49; Tavard, "Does the Protestant Ministry Have Sacramental Significance?" *Continuum* 6 (1968): 260–61; F. J. Beeck, "Towards an Ecumenical Understanding of the Sacraments," *Journal of Ecumenical Studies* 3 (1966): 57–112; Peter Bläser et al., *Amt und Eucharistie* (Paderborn: Bonifacius, 1973); Hans Küng, *The Church* (London: Burns & Oates, 1967), pp. 286, 443–44; J. M. R. Tillard, "Le votum eucharistiae: l'Eucharistie dans la rencontre des chrétiens," in *Miscellanea Liturgica in onore di Sua Eminenza il Cardinale G. Lercaro* (Rome, 1967), pp. 143–94; Tillard, "Catholiques romains et Anglicans: l'Eucharistie," *Nouvelle Revue Théologique* 93 (1971): 785–800; Maurice Villain, "Can There Be Apostolic Succession outside the Chain of Imposition of Hands?" in *Apostolic Succession: Rethinking a Barrier to Unity,* ed. Hans Küng, Concilium, vol. 34 (New York: Paulist Press, 1968), pp. 87–104; Joseph Duss-von Werdt, "What Can the Layman Do without the Priest?" in ibid., pp. 105–14; Bernard Sesboüé, *Serviteurs de l'Evangile: Les ministères dans l'Eglise* (Paris, 1971), pp. 115ff.; J. Flamand, *La fonction pastorale: ministère et sacerdoce au-delà de l'ecclésiologie du Vatican II* (Paris, 1970), pp. 19ff.; Ferdinand Klosterman, *Priester für Morgen* (Innsbruck: Tyrolia, 1970), pp. 89ff. See also all the essays in Edward Schillebeeckx and Johann-Baptist Metz, eds., *The Right of a Community to a Priest,* Concilium, vol. 133 (New York: The Seabury Press, 1980).

12. The most extensive study is by Legrand, "La présidence de l'Eucharistie selon la tradition ancienne," *Spiritus* 18 (1977): 409–31. Cf. A. Lemaire, "Ministère et Eucharistie aux origines de l'Eglise," *Spiritus* 18 (1977): 386–98. The most serious theological study is that of Edward Schillebeeckx, "The Christian Community and Its Office-Bearers," *The Right of a Community to a Priest,* pp. 95–133.

13. In *The Didache* [and other patristic writings], Ancient Christian Writers, no. 6, trans. James A. Kleist (Westminster, Md.: Newman, 1948), pp. 20–21, 23.

14. Ibid., pp. 23, 24.

15. Clement of Rome, "1 Corinthians 44:4–6" (in Ludwig Schopp et al., eds., *The Fathers of the Church*, vol. 1, *The Apostolic Fathers*, trans. Francis X. Glimm, Joseph M.-F. Marique, and Gerald G. Walsh [Washington, D.C.: Catholic University of America Press, 1962], p. 44).

16. Ignatius of Antioch, *To the Smyrnaeans,* ch. 8, vv. 3–4 (in Schopp, *Fathers of the Church,* 1:121).

17. Justin Martyr, *The First Apology,* cc. 65, 67 (in Schopp, *Fathers of the Church*, vol. 6, *Saint Justin Martyr,* trans. Thomas B. Falls, pp. 105, 107).

18. Hippolytus of Rome, *Traditio apostolica,* cc. 3, 4.

19. Ibid., ch. 3.

20. Tertullian, *Apology,* ch. 39, v. 5.

21. Tertullian, *De corona,* ch. 3, v. 5.

22. Tertullian, *De praescriptione,* ch. 41, v. 8.

23. Tertullian, *An Exhortation to Chastity,* ch. 7, v. 3 (in William P. Le Saint, trans., *Tertullian: Treatises on Marriage and Remarriage,* Ancient Christian Writers, no. 13 [Westminster, Md.: Newman, 1951], p. 53).

24. Tertullian, *De praescriptione*, ch. 41, vv. 5–8. Cf. G. Otranto, "Nonne est laici sacerdotes sumus? (Exhort. Cast. 7, 3)" *Vetera Christianorum* 8 (1971): 27–47.

25. Theodoret of Cyr, *The Ecclesiastical History*, book 1, ch. 22 (in Philip Schaff and Henry Wace, eds., *A Select Library of Nicene and Post-Nicene Fathers of the Christian Church,* 2nd series, vol. 3, *Theodoret, Jerome, Gennadius, Rufinus* [New York: Christian Literature; Oxford and London: Parker, 1892], p. 58).

26. Saint Cyprian of Carthage, Letters 65, ch. 1; 69, ch. 2; 72, ch. 2; *De unitate ecclesiae,* ch. 17 (in Alexander Roberts and James Donaldson, eds., *The Ante-Nicene Fathers,* vol. 5, *Fathers of the Third Century* [New York: Scribner's, 1899], pp. 367, 376, 380, 427).

27. Hippolytus of Rome, *Traditio apostolica*, ch. 9.

28. This is the conclusion reached by Legrand in "Présidence de l'Eucharistie."

29. Yves M.-J. Congar, "L'*ecclesia* ou communauté chrétienne, sujet intégral de l'action liturgique," in *La liturgie après Vatican II* (Paris, 1967), pp. 241–82.

30. *Translations and Reprints from the Original Sources of European History* (1900; reprint, Philadelphia: University of Pennsylvania, Department of History, n.d.), vol. 4, no. 2, p. 24.

31. Guerric d'Igny, *Sermon* 5 (*PL* 185:57).

32. Henricus Denzinger, ed., *Enchiridion Symbolorum*, nos. 794 (Innocent III, p. 257), 1084 (Fourth Lateran, p. 307), 1752 (Trent, p. 411).

33. Schillebeeckx, "The Christian Community."

34. Ibid., pp. 101–3.

35. Ibid., p. 103.

36. Ibid., pp. 105–6. Cf. B. Botte, "Secundi meriti munus," *Questions Liturgiques et Paroissiales* 21(1936): 84–88.

37. Schillebeeckx, "The Christian Community," pp. 110–14.

38. Tavard, "Protestant Ministry," p. 267.

39. Mansi 11:469. We find an exegesis of this canon in Beeck, "Towards an Ecumenical Understanding," pp. 81–86.

40. Denzinger, *Enchiridion Symbolorum,* no. 1290 (pp. 329–30); cf. nos. 1145 (pp. 313–14), 1146 (pp. 314–15), 1435 (p. 352).

41. For this whole complex problem, see Leonardo Boff, *Die Kirche als Sakrament im Horizont der Welterfahrung* (Paderborn: Bonifacius, 1972), pp. 377–412.

42. Congar, "*Supplet ecclesia:* propos en vue d'une théologie de l'économie dans la tradition latine," *Irénikon*, 1972, pp. 155–207.

43. *Presbyterorum Ordinis*, no. 2 (in Abbott, *Documents*, p. 535).

44. See L. Boff, "La conciencia mesiánica de Jesús: la presencia real en la Eucaristia; la sucesión apostólica," *Sal Terrae*, May 1982, pp. 394–401.

45. See the dramatic account of P. Domon in "Les premiers ministères dans l'Eglise de Corée," *Spiritus* 19 (1978): 62–75, which reads, in part: "Layman I Seung-Houn, 40, refounded the church in Korea in 1784. He organized a synodal, collegial structure, with ministries of evangelization, baptism, reconciliation, and Eucharist. He underwent instructions from the Jesuits of Peking, who had brought the Scriptures there. In 1786, after confession, the people unanimously begged him to celebrate the Eucharist. When the question of legitimacy was raised, I Seung-Houn being a layperson, all responded with one voice that not to celebrate the holy sacrifice meant to be deprived of spiritual nourishment, and to expose their salvation to an irreparable loss. . . . And he conferred this power on ten other persons in the community. At no time did I Seung-Houn cease to recognize the authority of the Church of Peking; but it happened that, in 1789, one of the ten who had been 'ordained,' having undertaken a theological study of the question, realized that, according to the prevailing norms approved by Pope Saint Gregory, they all had need of the sacrament of order, and alerted Seung-Houn of this. The latter, fearful of disturbing ecclesial communion, suspended the eucharistic celebrations, and wrote the bishop of Peking, explaining everything and begging mercy and understanding. The understanding was forthcoming. In 1794 he received a priest ordained in accordance with prevailing canons, and great was the joy of the community. Now: should we not distinguish the disciplinary problem from the theological one? Will these ten 'ordained' persons not have been extraordinary ministers of the Lord's Supper? Did they not bring Christ to the gathered community? Did they not do this sacramentally?"

7. *Quaestio Disputata* III

1. Cf. P. Müller, "Problème psychologique de la femme d'aujourd'hui," *Revue de Théologie et de Philosophie* 3 (1973): 237. Women were viewed as minors in need of protection, as servant-girls who were to be available but who had to be watched, as brides to be possessed exclusively, as spouses constantly dependent on their husbands, or as widows who were to stay with their children. In all circumstances, sex was the determining factor.

2. M. Versiani, "A mulher na Igreja: o fim de uma minoridade," *Jornal do Brasil*, May 7, 1973, p. B1. Georgia Harkness, *Woman in Church and Society* (Nashville: Abingdon, 1972), pp. 57–85. Rosemary Radford Ruether, *Religion and Sexism: Images of Woman in the Jewish and Christian Tradition* (New York: Simon and Schuster, 1974), pp. 117–83. Jean-Marie Aubert, *La mujer: antifeminismo y cristianismo* (Barcelona, 1976), pp. 53–90 (original: *La femme: antiféminisme et christianisme* [Paris: Cerf/Desclée, 1975]).

3. Cf. L. G. Quevedo, "Religiosas e tarefas presbiterais," *Convergência* 6 (1973): 149–63.

4. A. Leite, "A mulher na sociedade e na Igreja," *Brotéria* 97 (1973): 40–49. According to the *Annuario Pontificio* for 1973, there were twenty-one religious women working in pontifical commissions and the like.

5. See especially the appeal from Canadian women: "La femme dans l'Eglise et dans la société: mémoire des candiennes françaises à l'assemblée plénière de l'épiscopat canadien," *Eglise Canadienne* 4 (1971).

6. Cf. Versiani, *A mulher na Igreja,* p. 1, n. 2.

7. George B. Flahiff, "Sur les Ministères féminins dans l'Eglise," *Eglise Canadienne* 4 (1971): 286–87.

8. Arlene and Leonard Swidler, in their introduction to Haye van der Meer, *Women Priests in the Catholic Church? A Theological-Historical Investigation* (Philadelphia: Temple University Press, 1973), p. xxiv, citing *National Catholic Reporter*, Nov. 5, 1971.

9. Cf. SEDOC, 1973.

10. "A missão da mulher na Igreja," *Atualização* 42/43 (1973): 882; Arlene Swidler, *Woman in a Man's Church* (New York: Paulist Press, 1972).

11. Our principal sources here: Peter Ketter, *Christ and Womankind,* trans. Isabel McHugh (Westminster, Md.: Newman, 1952); Helga Rusche, *They Live by Faith: Women in the Bible,* trans. Elizabeth Williams (Baltimore: Helicon, 1963); "La conception chrétienne de la femme," *Lumière et Vie* 43 (1959), special issue; Herbert Braun, *Jesus of Nazareth: The Man and His Time,* trans. Everett R. Kalin (Philadelphia: Fortress Press, 1979); Leonard Swidler, "Jesus feminista," *Atualização* 42/43:876–80.

12. A. Oepke, *"Gunē,"* in Gerhard Kittel, ed., *Theological Dictionary of the New Testament,* trans. and ed. Geoffrey W. Bromiley, vol. 1, pp. 776–89; Paul Billerbeck, *Kommentar zum Neuen Testament aus Talmud und Midrasch,* vol. 3 (Munich, 1922–28), p. 558.

13. P. F. Sbik, *A voz masculina em honra da feminina* (Rio de Janeiro, 1972), p. 16.

14. Billerbeck, *Kommentar,* p. 468. Cf. Oepke, *"Gunē,"* pp. 781–82 (citing Sota, 3, 4; cf. the Babylonian Talmud, Sota, 21b).

15. Oepke, *"Gunē,"* p. 781 (citing the Jerusalem Talmud, Sota 10a:8).

16. Ibid., p. 777; Hans Lietzmann, *An die Galater* (Tübingen: Mohr, 1932), p. 23.

17. The bibliography here is enormous. We shall cite only some of the more significant books and articles: J. J. von Almen, "Est-il légitime de consacrer des femmes au ministère pastoral?" *Verbum Caro* 17 (1963): 26; Anonymous, "Warum nicht Priesterinnen?" *Der Grosse Entschluss* 21 (1966): 200–201; Alfred Bertholet, *Weibliches Priestertum* (Berlin, 1950); G. G. Blum, "Das Amt der Frau im Neuen Testament," *Novum Testamentum* 7 (1964): 142–61; M. Brunning, "Priestertum der Frau?" *Stimmen der Zeit* 176 (1964–65): 549–52; Georges Casalis, "L'Homme et la femme dans le ministère de l'Eglise," *Etudes Théologiques et Religieuses* 38 (1963): 27–46; Yves M.-J. Congar, "La femme dans l'Eglise," *Recherches des Sciences Philosophiques et Thèologiques* 37 (1953): 763–64; Jean Daniélou, "Les Ministères des femmes dans l'Eglise ancienne," *Maison Dieu* 61 (1960): 70–96; R. J. A. Eyden, "Die Frau im Kirchenamt: Pladoyer für die Revision einer traditionellen Haltung," *Wort und Wahrheit* 22 (1967): 350–62; P. Gallay, "Va-t-on vers un sacerdoce ministèriel des femmes dans l'Eglise catholique?" *Prêtre et Apôtre* 48 (1966): 247–48; Jean Galot, "L'accesso della donna ai ministeri della Chiesa," *Civiltà Cattolica* 123 (1973): 316–29; Santiago Giner Sempere, "La mujer y la potestad de orden: incapacidad de la mujer: argumentación histórica," *Revista Española de Derecho Canónico* 9 (1954): 841–69; A. M. Henry, "Les ministères de la femme dans l'Eglise," *Forma Gregis* 17 (1965): 95–110; J. Idígoras, "La femme dans l'ordre sacré," manuscript (Lima, 1963), or a résumé in *Informationes Catholiques Internationales,* no. 15 (November 1963), pp. 32–34, with further material in ibid., August 1965, pp. 29–39; E. Krebs, "Vom Priestertum der Frau," *Hochland* 19 (1922):

196–215; I. Müller and I. Raming, "Kritische Auseinandersetzung mit den Grüdnen der katholischen Theologie betreffend den Ausschluss der Frau vom sakramentalen Priestertum," in Gertrud Heinzelmann, ed., *Wir schweigen nicht länger! We Won't Keep Silence Any Longer!: Women Speak Out on Vatican Council II* (Zurich: Interfeminas, 1965), pp. 61–76; J. Sonnermans, "Vers l'ordination des femmes?" *Spiritus* 29 (1966): 403–22; van der Meer, *Women Priests?*; Roger Gryson, *The Ministry of Women in the Early Church,* trans. Jean Laporte and Mary Louise Hall (Collegeville, Minn.: Liturgical Press, 1976); P. Delhaye, "Rétrospective et prospective des ministères féminins dans l'Eglise," *Revue Théologique de Louvain* 3(1972): 55–75; B. Gherardini, "Donne in sacris?" *Seminarium* 6 (1966): 179–98; F. X. Remberger, "Priestertum der Frau?" *Theologie der Gegenwart* 9 (1966): 30–136; Elizabeth Gössmann, "Women as Priests?" in *Apostolic Succession: Rethinking a Barrier to Unity,* ed. Hans Küng, Concilium, vol. 34 (New York: Paulist Press, 1968), pp. 115–25; Jan Peters, "Is There Room for Women in the Functions of the Church?" in ibid., pp. 126–38; G. L. Quevedo, "Religiosas e tarefas," pp. 149–63, esp. pp. 159–61; J. Bodson, "La femme et le sacerdoce," *Vie Consacrée* 44 (1973): 332–69; Harkness, *Women in Church and Society*, pp. 205–20; Aubert, *La mujer*, pp. 171–210.

18. As in Galot, Gryson, von Almen, and others.

19. *Gaudium et Spes,* no. 9 (in Walter M. Abbott, ed., *The Documents of Vatican II* [New York: Herder and Herder and Herder, 1966], p. 25).

20. Ambrosiaster, *Commentarium in Epistolam ad Timotheum I,* ch. 3, no. 11 (*PL* 17:470).

21. For an exegesis of these texts see van der Meer, *Women Priests?*, pp. 10–45, esp. pp. 15–25; G. Dosselin, "Que la femme se taise dans l'assemblée," *Maison Dieu* 60 (1959): 183–92; Gottfried Fitzer, *Das Weib schweige in der Gemeinde: Überden unpaulinischen Charakter der mulier-taceat-Verse in 1. Korinther 14* (Munich: Kaiser, 1963); Galot, "L'accesso della donna," pp. 323ff.

22. Cf. F. P. Sola, *Sacrae Theologiae Summa,* BAC 73 (Madrid, 1953), 4:710.

23. Galot, "L'accesso della donna," p. 323; Gryson, *Ministry of Women;* Fitzer, *Das Weib schweige;* Hans Conzelmann, *1 Corinthians: A Commentary on the First Epistle to the Corinthians,* trans. James W. Leitch (Philadelphia: Fortress Press, 1975), p. 246, to name some of the authors who hold the interpolation thesis.

24. Van der Meer, *Women Priests?*, p. 87; I. Wilges, *A historia e doutrina de diaconato até o Concílio de Trento* (Rome: Antonianum, 1970); "As diaconisas," *Convergência* 6 (1973): 352–60.

25. Van der Meer, *Women Priests?*, p. 93, citing *PL* 59:55, among other references.

26. Ibid., p. 88.

27. C. Koser, "De sacerdotio beatae Mariae Virginis," *Maria et Ecclesia,* vol. 2 (Rome, 1959), pp. 169–206.

28. Daniélou cited by Quevedo, "Religiosas e tarefas presbyterais," p. 161.

29. These experiments have not escaped a critical analysis on the part of theology. See, e.g., G. Deintze, "Amt der Pastorin," *Evangelische Theologie* 22 (1962): 509–35; E. Hertzsch, "Das Problem der Ordination der Frau in der Evangelischen Kirche," *Theologische Literaturzentung* 81 (1956): 379–82; F. R. Refoulé, "Les Problèmes de femmes prêtres en Suède," *Lumière et Vie* 43 (1959): 65–99; Concilium General Secretariat, "Women's Place in the Ministry of Non-Catholic Christian Churches," in *Apostolic Succession: Rethinking a Barrier to Unity,* ed. Hans Küng, Concilium, vol. 34 (New York: Paulist Press, 1968), pp. 163–77.

30. Eyden, "Frau im Kirchenamt," p. 357, cited in Gössmann, "Women as Priests?", p. 121.

31. Gössmann, "Women as Priests?", p. 122–23.

32. Cf. Eyden, "Frau im Kirchenamt," pp. 350–62; Karl Rahner, *Theological Investigations,* vol. 8, trans. David Bourke (New York: Seabury Press, 1977), pp. 75–93.

33. Principal bibliography: Leonardo Boff, "O sacerdócio: vocação e missão de todos os leigos por modos diferentes," in *O Destino do homem e do mundo* (Petrópolis, Brazil: Vozes, 1973), pp. 85–125; *Teología del sacerdocio,* vols. 1–4 (Burgos: Aldecoa, 1972), with contributions by outstanding specialists; *Der priesterliche Dienst,* vols. 1–6 (Freiburg: Herder, 1970), also presenting the contribution of the best German writers; Bonaventura Kloppenburg, *The Priest: Living Instrument and Minister of Christ the Eternal Priest,* trans. Matthew J. O'Connell (Chicago: Franciscan Herald, 1974); Urbano Zilles, *A diaconia dos presbíteros na Igreja em realização* (Petrópolis, Brazil: Vozes, 1972), pp. 69–107. See also the particularly rich bibliography compiled by Juan Esquerda Bifet at the end of each volume of *Teología del sacerdocio.*

34. Boff, "O sacerdócio," pp. 90–98, and bibliography.

35. *Lumen Gentium,* no. 10 (in Abbott, *Documents,* p. 27).

36. Ibid., *Apostolicam Actuositatem,* no. 3 (in Abbott, *Documents*).

37. *Documentos Pontifícos,* no. 183 (Petrópolis, Brazil: Vozes, 1972).

38. *Presbyterorum Ordinis,* no. 5 (in Abbott, *Documents,* p. 541).

39. This is the approach taken by the German Bishops' Synod, "Schwerpunkte des priesterlichen Dienstes," *Herderkorrespondenz* 26 (1972): 86–91; cf. the French bishops', "Le ministère du prêtre," *Documentation Catholique* 55 (1972): 32–35; cf. also A. Kasper, "Die Kirche und ihre Amter," *Glaube und Geschichte* (Mainz, 1970), pp. 355–70.

40. Cf. Congar, "Quelques problèmes touchant les ministères," *Nouvelle Revue Théologique* 93 (1971): 785–800, esp. p. 793; G. H. Tavard, "The Function of the Minister in the Eucharistic Celebration," *Journal of Ecumenical Studies* 4 (1967): 629–49; Joseph Duss-von Werdt, "What Can the Layman Do without the Priest?", in *Apostolic Succession: Rethinking a Barrier to Unity,* pp. 105–14.

41. *Translations and Reprints from the Original Sources of European History* (1900; reprint, Philadelphia: University of Pennsylvania, Department of History, n.d.), vol. 4, no. 2, p. 24.

42. Rahner, "Priestertum der Frau?" *Stimmen der Zeit,* May 1977, pp. 291–301.

43. Ibid., p. 300.

Index

Compiled by James Sullivan